In praise of *How to Find a GOOD Job in 90 Days*

A fast read, with tons of practical advice. This book shows you how to conduct a GOOD job search without making any of the typical mistakes.

> Maureen Crawford Hentz, U.S. Manager of
> Talent Acquisition, Diversity & Compliance,
> OSRAM SYLVANIA INC. (a Siemens company)

No matter what we set out to accomplish in life, we need a vision of what success will look like, a plan to get there, and the fortitude to persist through all the challenges. Jim and Kathy's *How to Find a GOOD Job in 90 Days* will lead you not only to a new job but to an opportunity where you can truly make a difference doing something that interests you.

> Tom Welch, "America's Career Coach",
> Executive Coach to America's leaders, and
> author of *Work Happy Live Healthy*

Finally!! A job search book that really tackles the problems, solutions, strategies and process in a concise and powerfully presented product. As a Career Counselor I have reviewed countless books on the subject. This is definitely one of the best out there. For someone struggling with the practical issues of finding not just a job, but the RIGHT and GOOD job, this is a field guide with value. Thank you Kathy and Jim!

> Edith M. Donohue, PhD and co-author, *Life After Layoff*

I once invited an unemployed candidate to meet with me to interview and discuss a job opportunity we were representing. Despite her interest, she was so busy with networking appointments that she couldn't fit me into her schedule! *How to Find a GOOD Job in 90 Days* is a really helpful tool to keep job seekers focused on the important priorities of finding a "Good Job" and staying on track. An easy read, the book covers all the basics and should be in the library of anyone pursuing a job transition.

>Donna L. Friedman, Chair & CEO, Tower Consultants, Ltd. Executive Search

---

Jim and Kathy guide the reader well toward combining the practical and the personal. As *How to Find a GOOD Job in 90 Days* coaches, you must have organization and process skills to accomplish your goals, but you must also be sure you really know yourself. An easy read, with plenty of gems for advancing one's career on the executive track.

>Marc D. Lewis, CEO, Leadership Capital Group (retained executive search for information intense business)

How to Find a *GOOD* Job in 90 Days
The 5 Step Guide to a Successful Job Search

Jim Stokely and Kathy Shabotynskyj

Copyright © 2009 by James Rorex Stokely III and Kathy Shabotynskyj

All rights reserved. Except as permitted under the U.S. Copyright Act of 1976, no part of this book may be reproduced, distributed, or transmitted in any form by any means, electronic or mechanical, including photocopying, recording or by any other information storage and retrieval system, except brief excerpts for the purpose of review, without written permission from the publisher.

PUBLISHER: Burnett, Cole and Irving
P.O. Box 550
Hamilton, MA 01936

E-mail: goodjob@mycareerteam.com

Visit our web site at www.mycareerteam.com

Burnett, Cole and Irving books may be purchased for business or sales promotional use. For information please write the publisher. You can also visit the author's website at www.mycareerteam.com to order individual copies.

PUBLISHER'S NOTE: This publication is designed to provide accurate and authoritative information in regard to the subject matter covered. However, neither the publisher nor the co-authors guarantee the accuracy, adequacy, or completeness of any information provided, and are not responsible for any errors or omissions or the results obtained from use of such information.

ISBN: 978-0-615-31074-9

Library of Congress Control Number: 2009907827

Printed in the United States of America

First Edition

dedication

Jim Stokely
To my daughter Elizabeth, who read this book and landed her first GOOD job in 47 days.

Kathy Shabotynskyj
To my husband Tony, who has steadfastly encouraged me during every job change and has enthusiastically supported my writing this book. And to each and every job seeker, this book can be your job search bible; I hope it brings you great success.

Table of Contents

Introduction	5
Month One: REST and PREP	11
Step One: **REST**	
Chapter One: R is for REFLECTION	14
Chapter Two: E is for EDUCATION	21
Chapter Three: S is for SCHEDULE	29
Chapter Four: T is for TOGETHERNESS	37
Step Two: **PREP**	
Chapter Five: P is for PURPOSE	41
Chapter Six: R is for RESUME	49
Chapter Seven: E is for EQUIPMENT	66
Chapter Eight: P is for PERSONAL REFERENCES	72
Month Two: SHARE and HUNT	78
Step Three: **SHARE**	
Chapter Nine: S is for SOCIAL NETWORKING	80
Chapter Ten: H is for HEALTH and HAPPINESS	84
Chapter Eleven: A is for the ABC's of the INFORMATION MEETING	88
Chapter Twelve: R is for RESULTS TRACKING and ACTION PLANNING	93
Chapter Thirteen: E is for ETIQUETTE	100
Step Four: **HUNT**	
Chapter Fourteen: H is for HEADHUNTERS	106
Chapter Fifteen: U is for UNLOCKING the WANT ADS	115
Chapter Sixteen: N is for NETWORKING	120
Chapter Seventeen: T is for TARGETED EMPLOYERS	129
Month Three and Step Five : **FIND**	139
Chapter Eighteen: F is for FOCUS	140
Chapter Nineteen: I is for INTERVIEW	144
Chapter Twenty: N is for NEGOTIATE	155
Chapter Twenty-One: D is for DECIDE	164
CONCLUSION	170

Introduction

Our book is for anyone who is considering a new job. If you are currently working or recently unemployed, or reevaluating your career in anticipation of a new position, this book will be a great tool for an effective and efficient job search. For those who are completing school and will soon be searching for a job, our manual will serve you now and for your entire career. For anyone wanting a job or a new job, here is an action guide designed to lead you simply and quickly toward a GOOD job. Ninety days or three months is our standard for "quickly."

What distinguishes a GOOD job from a mere job? Essentially, a GOOD job is a job that you want. A more precise definition will become clearer as you read this book.

Timing is another main ingredient of this career guide. This 90-day way to a good job leads you, "the candidate," through five distinct steps: REST, PREP, SHARE, HUNT and FIND. These five acronyms will reveal the most essential information to make your pursuit of a new position a strategic and successful initiative. Each of 21 chapters outlined below takes you further along an efficient and effective path through the world of transition. In a targeted and strategic approach, you can land your next position. The difference between our guide and other similar guides is that we cover more than the resume, or interviewing, or negotiating a job offer. We cover the whole waterfront, A to Z. In a thorough and insightful way, you will complete your job search following the 5 steps:

REST
Take two weeks to rest and think.

- **Chapter One: R**eflection
  Choose your preferred career.

- **Chapter Two: E**ducation
  Determine whether you need additional education.

- **Chapter Three: S**chedule
  Start following a new and improved daily schedule.

- **Chapter Four: T**ogetherness
  Enlist a loved one to help you in your job search.

PREP
Take another two weeks to assemble some items critical to the search.

- **Chapter Five: P**urpose
  Define your job objective – your preferred job type.

- **Chapter Six: R**esume
  Prepare a resume that supports your job objective.

- **Chapter Seven: E**quipment
  Assemble a few key pieces of home office equipment.

- **Chapter Eight: P**ersonal References
  Identify the right people who can and will attest to your value as an employee.

SHARE
Start talking to the right people in the right way.

- **Chapter Nine: S**ocial Networking
  Establish an internet presence and use social network sites.

- **Chapter Ten: H**ealth
  Stay confident and upbeat.

- **Chapter Eleven: A**BC's of the Information Meeting
  List all the people you know and talk to most of them.

- **Chapter Twelve: R**esults Tracking & Action Planning
  Track your results and start making weekly action plans.

- **Chapter Thirteen: E**tiquette
  Check your handshake, eye contact, and table manners.

HUNT
Utilize headhunters, job sites, networking, and targeted employers.

- **Chapter Fourteen: H**eadhunters
  Establish relationships with headhunters in your field.

- **Chapter Fifteen: U**nlocking the Want Ads
  Check want ads and internet job sites.

- **Chapter Sixteen: N**etworking
  Reach out to your contacts daily and gather leads.

- **Chapter Seventeen: T**argeted Employers
  Identify some specific possible employers and contact them.

FIND
Focus on specific job opportunities and land the right one for you.

- **Chapter Eighteen: F**ocus
  If an organization expresses interest in you, find out more about it and give it priority.

- **Chapter Nineteen: I**nterview
  Prepare for telephone and on-site interviewing.

- **Chapter Twenty: N**egotiate
  Analyze a job offer and pitch a counteroffer.

- **Chapter Twenty-one: D**ecide
  Determine which of several offers is right for you.

Ninety days is a realistic target. Some will accomplish a job change faster; others may take a prolonged approach. When you factor in the economic recession dating back to December 2007, which has influenced every industry, the challenge of landing a GOOD job that much more daunting. Understand that it will take action on your part to overcome the obstacles. This guide will take you on a directed course toward a new job. It will be up to you to follow these steps and create your own success. The five steps over 90 days will overlap, and if you follow the guide, you will actually enjoy your search for a new job.

5 STEPS	MONTH ONE	MONTH TWO	MONTH THREE
REST	=====>		
PREP	=====>		
SHARE		============	=====>
HUNT		=========	========>
FIND			===========>

Jim's Story

I know, because I've been in the world of transition. Ten years out of college, I changed careers. I returned to school and, afterwards, took a corporate job. Five years later, I changed companies. Four years after that, I was terminated from the company. This book sprang from the job search I then pursued. It summarizes the lessons I learned from that search and from my other transitions. It also incorporates my 20 years of experience as a human resources director in two multi-billion dollar companies.

Kathy's Insights

Me, too. I know transition. I've worked in the corporate, private, public and non-profit sectors in Recreation, Association Management, and Human Resources. I change careers every ten years or so. My contributions to this action guide come from personal and professional experiences, making my own career choices, and career coaching others to new jobs. This book covers the basics and will not mire the job seeker in vast reading and exercises. It is focused on actions and results. This guide will assist you as if you had a career coach in your corner – and now you have two.

Everyone changes jobs. A Department of Labor report on career myths debunks the myth that there is *one* perfect job with this argument:

> Reality: There are many occupations—and many jobs—that you would enjoy. Focusing on finding a single, perfect career is not only intimidating, it's limiting. If you're like most people, you will have several jobs and careers in your life, and each will have positive and negative aspects to it. Furthermore, your job preferences are apt to change over time as you gain

experience, skill, and self-knowledge. Keeping your options open is a position of strength, not weakness. [1]

You will change your job either voluntarily or involuntarily throughout your life. The lessons on how to do it are contained in this book. They include three underlying principles which remain in the background of this book, but which inform all five steps. The principles are these:

- You must come to know what you want.
- You should approach the months between one job and another as a valuable and desirable time, an opportunity to explore multiple interests and to draw closer to family and friends.
- You should conduct a rifled and targeted search rather than a broadcast and shotgun search.

We hope this book will be your best entry to your job search -- and your best exit from it.

---

[1] Occupational Outlook Quarterly (U.S. Department of Labor: Fall 2005)

Month One: REST and PREP

In this first month of your job search, you will REST and PREP. Weeks one and two must be devoted to Rest, including (1) career planning, (2) considering training and development (or further education), (3) planning your daily routine, and (4) including a loved one in your search. Other than a bit of library research, you can complete all of these activities at home.

None of these steps requires you to sell yourself to anybody, or to persuade anybody of anything. You need a rest from the recent grind. Even if you are still gainfully employed, you need time to step back and think about a few things: your life's work and accomplishments, your needs for effective learning and for a productive routine, your relationship with the person closest to you. Once you gain some perspective and direction with regard to these, you'll have done yourself a great and crucial favor.

Weeks three and four constitute the PREP or preparation phase. Now is the time to focus on (1) a clear direction or objective, (2) a professional resume that will support that direction, (3) having the equipment necessary to execute your search, and (4) identifying your references.

> **Jim's Story**
>
> An interviewer who once denied me a job said to me, "If you don't know where you're going, you'll never get there." He was trying to tell me something. I believe his intended message involved me sitting down and thinking for a while: "Is this what I want to do for the rest of my working life? Can I figure out a better way to fit my interests and skills with my vocation?"

This is actually the fun phase of finding a GOOD job. It is your time to concentrate on you. Now you will take control of your future by assessing your past accomplishments and inventory of skills, and by identifying your passions that will lead the way to a clear career objective.

> **Kathy's Insights**
>
> Whatever the circumstances surrounding your search for a new position, don't take the ready, shoot, aim approach. The best way to shoot yourself in the foot is to reach out to all your best career contacts and give them a wrong or an ill-prepared message: "I lost my job; let me know if you hear of anything." You will be a burden to those individuals, and you haven't given them enough information for them to effectively help you. Sure, the wolves may be at your door, but don't panic; this methodical approach to a career change works. Follow the process and you can land a GOOD job, the right job, and you will land faster than anyone who follows the ready, shoot, aim approach.

Jim's Story

I once knew a good carpenter who was also an alcoholic. His life veered between jobs well done and drinking binges that lasted for days at a time. He experienced many high points in his career -- beautiful constructions and heartfelt compliments -- and he also sank to many lows. But the lowest I ever saw him was a few days after he had sold his tools for liquor. If I had run across him the day after the sale, he would have been happily intoxicated. When I did catch up with him, he was without hope because he didn't have the tools he needed to get hired.

Do not discount the tools of your job search. You need a clear idea of your job objective, a resume that says exactly who you are, the equipment to maximize your efficiency, and a set of personal references. By the end of the first month of your search, with these in place, you will be well on your way to finding a GOOD job.

R is for REFLECTION

During these first two weeks of your job search, you should do some career planning. We define a career as a field of activity which can support a working life. Depending on your financial and other needs, viable careers can range from research to accounting to printing books to management consulting to manufacturing glass.

The primary objective of your reflection is to go from a variety of possible careers, depending on your aptitudes and desires, to a preferred career. Graphically, your progression in this chapter looks something like this:

Test possible careers...

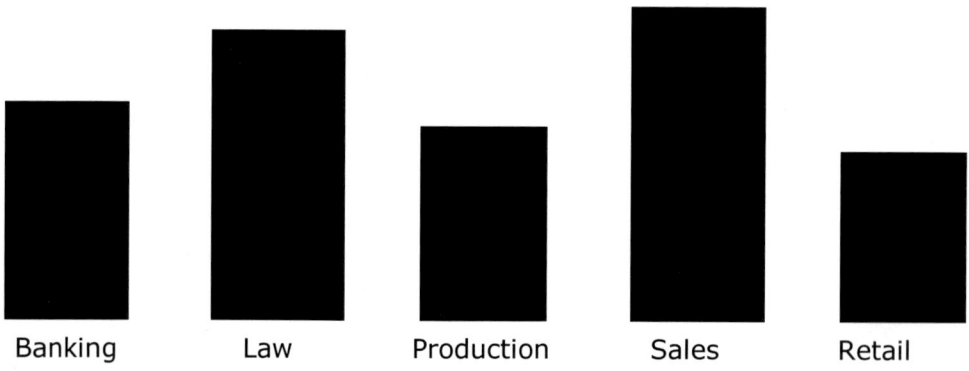

...and choose a preferred career:

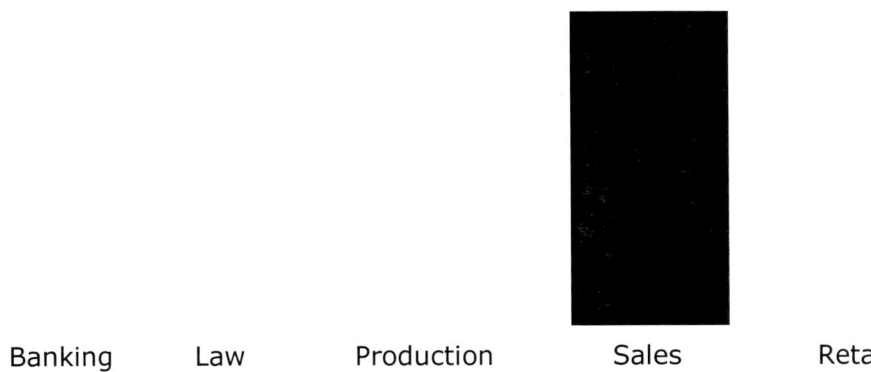

   Banking   Law   Production   Sales   Retail

Each career choice is measured, and the one with the highest ranking is your preferred career. The heights of the career bars vary because your potential career level will vary depending on aptitude, desire, demonstrated skills, and employment circumstances.

You probably have experience right now in one or more fields of activity. You may be in mid-career, having already achieved a certain career level. A key question for you is whether to change careers or stay in your current career. If you know you will stay, you might as well skip the rest of this chapter. The issues discussed here will only hassle you, and you want to spend your energy maximizing prospects in your current career.

If you think you may want to change careers, you might identify possible careers through a pair of approaches:

      (1)   List all the careers you have given serious thought to in recent years, no matter how fleeting that thought may have been. Other people you love and/or respect may have suggested careers to you. A useful introduction to careers is <u>the Professional Careers Sourcebook: An Information</u>

<u>Guide for Career Planning</u> (edited by Kathleen M. Savage and Charity Anne Dorgan, Detroit: Gale Research). The Sourcebook profiles over 100 careers and lists sources that describe career jobs, salaries and requirements. This volume also lists basic books about the field, so that you can gain a sense for job content and challenge.

(2) Sign up for aptitude testing or for career coaching. Many psychologists, campus centers, and career coaches offer such services. One useful resource is the Internet Career Connection developed by James C. Gonyea (http://www.iccweb.com). A free self-instructional program, the Career Selection and Planning Guide, is available online, as is a shorter Perfect Career Interest Inventory.

You can find a career coach in your community or online to help you determine an appropriate path. Often you will find career coaches listed in the yellow pages under Resume Services, as that is typically one outcome of a career coaching engagement.

After you have identified possible careers, test them against each other by using the following checklist:

Career Checklist

- ☐ Possible career:
  _____
  (Choose one of your possible careers and write it in the blank space.)

- ☐ Is this my current career, or is it another career?
  (If you are testing your current career, jump to the question about money; if you are testing another career, ask yourself the next question about education.)

- Do I need further education to make this career possible?

- Can I make enough money in this line of work?
  (If this is your current career and the answer is no, go back to the question about education; further education may change your answer.)

- Does this career offer sufficient opportunity for advancement?
  (If this is your current career and the answer is no, go back to the question about education; further education may change your answer.)

- Will this career be workable for the family?

- How much do I want to pursue this career?

Let's look more closely at the questions on this checklist.

Do I Need Further Education to Make This Career Possible?

Virtually all careers nowadays require evidence of education: some sort of degree or certification. The classic professions -- medicine and law -- are prime examples of this.

Educational requirements evolve for some careers. For example, high school teaching used to require a slew of education courses. But with school systems around the country recognizing a whole new talent pool in disaffected corporate managers, teacher education standards are now recognizing life experience more than in the past.

To determine if you need further education, you might return to the Professional Careers Sourcebook. For most possible careers, this book lists certification agencies and their courses of study. If you do need further education, that need could be the major factor in your decision to pursue or abandon this career possibility. One book that is helpful when determining your future career direction is The Enhanced Guide for

Occupational Exploration (JIST Works, Inc.) This catalogue includes descriptions for over 2,800 jobs and each one includes a general educational development code to indicate the complexity of skill needed for the position and also an Academic Code that refers to the educational degree required.

Can I Make Enough Money in This Line of Work?

This may seem like a crass question to ask, but it is a valid screen. We are talking about your working life instead of your hobby, your vocation rather than your avocation. Many factors influence your pay, including the state of the economy, the costs of living and labor in a geographical area, the size and solvency of your company, your job responsibilities, and your individual performance. Another factor is the particular industry in which you are working. Pay levels by industry vary from year to year, but historical patterns do emerge. For example, on a job-for-job basis, pay in the oil, chemical and pharmaceutical industries has tended to be higher than pay in most other industries. Bank salaries were significantly lower than manufacturing salaries in the early 1980s, but by the early 1990s total cash pay (salary plus targeted bonus) at financial institutions had generally caught up with total cash paid by manufacturers.

We all read about CEO pay in the major business magazines every spring after most company proxies are published. Pay is also surveyed for many other jobs down through the typical corporation. Trade periodicals sometimes conduct their own surveys. Compensation consulting firms conduct numerous surveys for industries, functional areas, and/or geographic locations. A guide to some of these surveys by career type is the Professional's Job Finder by Daniel Lauber (River Forest, Illinois: Planning / Communications). Also, WorldatWork (www.worldatwork.org, formerly the American Compensation Association) regularly lists a variety of pay surveys. Salary.com is an online option that offers a free service to benchmark your job to the closest match in their database by searching your job title and location. It is a useful tool to understand typical job functions and the salary range for that position. Additional services are offered for nominal fees.

Jim's Story

In my most recent job search, I seriously considered a return to the non-profit world of museums, colleges, and so forth. However, after scanning salary offers in The New York Times week after week, I must admit that I decided against non-profit primarily for monetary reasons.

Kathy's Insights

Contemplate not only the work you are going to do, where will you do it, and with whom you will be working, but consider the quality of life you can afford with certain careers. There are tradeoffs with most career situations, and you must choose your comfort level with the risk vs. reward of your desired career path.

Does This Career Offer Sufficient Opportunity for Advancement?

Any field of activity offers a variety of jobs and career levels. As a general rule, longer experience and/or more education in the field will result in a higher career level. This means that time is required to climb the ladder from, say, entry-level accountant to senior accountant to general accounting manager to assistant controller to controller. In many cases, your career will not grow straight up the rungs of a ladder so much as laterally into a related field, then crisscross upward in the manner of a lattice. However, make sure that an enticing job in a new field does not require too much preparatory work for your stage in life.

Will This Career Be Workable for the Family?

Read "family" as family and/or loved ones, including parents and relatives. Proximity to family or friends may be very important to you, and some careers mix less well with family than do others. Many consultants, for example, travel more than 75% of their time. If you have young children and go into consulting, don't expect to tuck them in bed every night, or coach their soccer team. Many corporate positions might force you to relocate one or more times.

If, after thought and investigation, it just seems too difficult to put together the pieces of a workable family life for a particular career, choose another one. The point is to think of your next career move holistically. Consider the work, the career advancement potential, the work/life balance, and the pay.

How Much Do I Want to Pursue This Career?

Your possible career can successfully clear the education, money, career advancement, and family hurdles through simple yes or no answers. If it does meet these thresholds, then you are ready to give a score to your possible career on the basis of what really counts: how much you want to do it.

Give yourself a score on this single dimension by thinking about your future frame of mind when commuting to work. Picture yourself five years after landing your job, and if you can't believe that someone is actually paying you to do what you would do anyway, give yourself a 10. If you see yourself as pressed against the wall, underpaid and overworked, fearful that you won't be able to live up to expectations, give yourself a 1. Your score will probably fall somewhere between these two extremes.

The point here is pretty much to go with your gut. Joseph Campbell, a lifelong scholar of human aspirations as revealed through myths and mythmaking, advised young persons seeking their life's work to "Follow your bliss." This wise counsel holds for older folks, too.

SUCCESS GAUGE
You have mastered R is for Reflection if:
You believe in the viability of your career choice and see yourself landing a GOOD job!

E is for EDUCATION

One of your big decisions at this point in finding a new job is determining if you need to return to school. If you are still employed and contemplating a return to school you must consider the adjustments you will have to make in your time allocation. If you are between jobs and are leaning toward a new career, there will never be a better time to acquire the necessary education. This is so because of two reasons. First, you are younger now than you ever will be again. Second, you are at a natural transition point in your life. Of course, you and your family (if you have a spouse and/or children) must make this decision together. Time management issues come to the fore, and a spouse may need to go to work or add a second job. Children need to understand the proposed changes and be allowed to support a family life that may include less parental attention.

Whatever you decide, you will need information about your educational options in order to make good decisions. This chapter helps guide you to that information. In so doing, it addresses two primary types of education: (1) post-high school education to prepare oneself for a new career; and (2) education within a given career, oriented toward career development.

Education for Career Preparation

This kind of education embraces both the liberal arts model and the vocational training model. College, university, and graduate education fall into this category.

If you don't have a 2-year or 4-year college degree, establish an action plan to get one. The degree that makes the most sense for your near-term career progression might be an associate's degree from a community college. These 2-year institutions have generally become very good at transferring technical skills that are worth something in the marketplace. Such skills, which range from computer network administration to various forms of medical therapy, can lead to stable positions in the lower to middle tiers of a company. <u>Peterson's Guide to Two-Year Colleges</u> (Princeton, NJ: Peterson's Guides) contains profiles and in-depth descriptions of over 1,400 colleges nationwide. This volume includes an article on "Returning to School: A Guide for Adult Students," a table of colleges by state, a grouping of majors by broad career, and listings of Associate Degree programs at 4-year as well as 2-year colleges.

Upper-level corporate positions typically require at least a 4-year degree. The 4-year college experience for 18-to-21-year olds once defined life on college campuses. Times have changed since the 1970s and 1980s. Over the past 25 years, the proportion of college students older than 24 has increased from one-fourth to one-half. Today, there is a wide variety of recognized routes to a liberal arts degree, many of which take more than four years, may be combined with work, and are designed for students much older than the legal drinking age. There are more than 3,000 colleges, universities, technical institutes, junior colleges, seminaries, and other institutions of higher education in the United States. <u>Lovejoy's College Guide</u> (Edited by Charles T. Straughn II and Barbarasue Lovejoy Straughn, New York: Lovejoy's College Guide) provides comprehensive descriptions of your school choices and is updated annually. Be sure to review the Career Curricula Index which "lists more than 500 career-related fields, from Accounting through Zoology, and the institutions where they are taught."

A 4-year degree is generally necessary for graduate school. The typical business school program takes 2 years, law school 3, and medical school more.

Jim's Story

I can attest to the value of business school. Ten years out of college, I decided to change careers. I attended business school for two years, discovered a new career interest, received my MBA (Master of Business Administration), and saw my salary go up by 64%. As difficult as the cost of tuition and the interruption in income were for me and my wife, our investment in education was definitely worth the sacrifice.

With the right choice of program, any of the above levels of education can be achieved in conjunction with a current job. In most cases, though, this entails a longer period of study. In any case, financial aid may be an issue. Gale Research periodically updates a volume called <u>Scholarships, Fellowships, and Loans: A Guide to Education-Related Financial Aid Programs for Students and Professionals</u> (Edited by Debra M. Kirby, Detroit: Gale Research). This guide describes over 3,300 sources of aid, and provides indexes by vocational goals, field of study, and requirements for legal residence, place of study, gender, ethnicity, and/or organizational affiliation.

Another source of educational funding may be your state's employment/unemployment agency. Often there are federal and state funds available for retraining. Workers who have been totally or partially separated from their jobs because of increased foreign imports may be eligible for assistance under the Trade Adjustment Assistance/Trade Readjustment Allowances programs. The Trade Adjustment Assistance program can provide benefits associated with training, job search, relocation allowances, and other reemployment services.

Kathy's Insights

If adding additional educational credentials is one of your goals, you would benefit by seeking those employers who subsidize educational advancement as one of their benefits. Often employers offer this incentive to develop their employees and add bench strength and competencies in specific job functions where the talent pool is particularly narrow. Nursing and engineering are two occupations where it is a common practice of employers to subsidize educational advancement, but many corporations offer some education benefits.

Education for Career Development

During the 1950's and 1960's, with American business dominating most world markets, training and managerial development were luxuries. An executive with a sound college degree -- or almost any advanced degree -- could stay with the same corporation throughout their career. In the absence of widespread computer systems, managers were needed if for no other reason than to handle the flow of information from one department to another.

Today, computer networks have rendered obsolete the manager-as-information-conduit. In order to assure a career that provides adequate financial support and emotional rewards, the successful manager of the 21st century must acquire and maintain a variety of skills (defined as demonstrated abilities). Relevant sets of skills span the gamut from technical skills to interpersonal and other managerial skills. A short list of such skills reads as follows:

- Understanding the business
- Understanding the organization
- Listening
- Responding to the customer
- Making persuasive presentations
- Writing clearly
- Analyzing complex problems

- Acting with incomplete information
- Taking calculated risks
- Taking charge as needed
- Partnering with key executives
- Adapting
- Building support for an innovation
- Leading change

This list is incomplete, but you get the drift. Many companies refer to skills critical to their growth as "core competencies." The important thing to remember about these competencies is that they are developed throughout one's career. More and more companies are rewarding an employee's growth in competencies with salary increases and promotional opportunities. At many companies today, your career will not grow unless you understand the fundamentals of the business.

How can you strengthen yourself in these important skill sets? Numerous means are available to you, most of which fall into one of four categories:

- Training outside the company
- Training within the company
- On-the-job training
- Career development activities

Let's look briefly at each of these categories.

Training Outside the Company

Certification varies in importance from career to career. At the high end, the Certified Public Accountant (CPA) designation is widely recognized as a sign of expertise, and it remains valuable in the marketplace. A typical certification program might involve a handful of structured courses, each several days long, taken over a multi-year period by workers in that career.

As mentioned in the Reflection chapter, the <u>Professional Careers Sourcebook</u> lists certification agencies for over 100 careers. Compared to college or graduate school, certification generally represents less of a sacrifice in terms of time or money. But certification still requires significant spurts of energy in addition to work. The positive returns can far outweigh the investment.

Many other non-certification training programs are available. The American Society of Training and Development, a 50-year old association with over 50,000 members, can be a starting point for your exploration of such programs. Based in Alexandria, Virginia, the ASTD maintains -- among its many offerings -- a database of over 100,000 training-related products and/or programs.

Training Inside the Company

The larger the company, the more likely it is to have some sort of internal training program administered out of the human resources, information systems, and/or sales functions. If you are not in sales, ask sales management if you can take the orientation program designed for sales representatives. If it exists, this kind of program gives valuable insights into the company's products and channels of distribution. Information systems workshops will keep you updated on needed software, both internally designed and packaged by external vendors. Human resources offerings tend to concentrate on generic management skills and regulatory compliance issues; you should choose these to fill gaps in your core competencies.

Take advantage, too, of self-study resources offered by the company. These might include online tutorials, books, audio tapes for your commute, and integrated kits combining a self-instructional workbook with audio-visual support. Although self-study is not the most effective training method in some areas, it has proven effective as a supplement to live instruction. Two attractive benefits of this course of study are the minimal cost of company programs and the ability to learn at your own pace.

On-the-Job Training

Senior executives will tell you that their most significant career development experiences resulted from moving into a new and bigger job, a different job in the same area, or an augmented job with an added area or two of responsibility. Such moves demand a sharp learning curve for immediate results, and the learners are generally highly motivated to make it happen. In your current job (or your next job), you should discuss with your supervisor the possibilities of such job changes. Keep your eyes open for opportunities to serve on task forces, or interdepartmental teams, that can expose you to unfamiliar areas of the company and leaders from other pieces of the business who can become part of your network of career contacts. If you run across a task force that interests you, request to serve on it now or at the next member rotation.

Kathy's Insights

It may be fun to plan the company picnic or annual holiday party, but realistically, these activities are perceived as lightweight and low priorities to the company's bottom line. Use participation on these planning committees as a gateway to higher level task forces.

Career Development Activities

Some activities are specifically oriented toward career development. Annual development planning with your supervisor is usually included at performance appraisal time. A human resources manager may be available to counsel you concerning your career development and future advancement potential. Some companies run full-fledged management assessment centers, where your behavior in group exercises is closely observed, analyzed, and fed back to you for development purposes. A less intense experience is the 360-degree assessment, in which you select several subordinates and colleagues to give you anonymous feedback about your competencies. Survey responses from these persons as well as your supervisor are collected and reported to you, with your "scores" compared to those of other managers in the company, industry, and country.

Most companies today point to you as the person primarily responsible for your career development. The company can make resources available to you, and can even develop career plans with you, but at the bottom line, you must take charge of your own career. Ironically for the company, this sometimes means changing companies, which is what this book is all about.

SUCCESS GAUGE:
You have mastered E is for Education if:
You have determined (1) you do not need additional education, or (2) you do need additional education and have chosen the program, institution and funding source(s).

S is for SCHEDULE

After you have reflected on your life priorities, including possible further education, you need a daily routine. You say you already have one? Well...you need one suited to this transitional period.

The schedule you are now following is probably built around your current or most recent job and may look something like this:

6:00 AM - 7:30 AM:	Out of bed, shower, breakfast, newspaper
7:30 AM - 8:00 AM:	Commute to work
8:00 AM - Noon:	Work
Noon - 1:00 PM:	Lunch at or near work
1:00 PM - 6:00 PM:	Work
6:00 PM - 6:30 PM:	Commute from work
6:30 PM - 8:00 PM:	Supper
8:00 PM -10:00 PM:	Relax, television, reading, to bed

This is a perfect daily routine for the kind of person the philosopher Herbert Marcuse termed a "one dimensional man." Out of 16 waking hours, 11 involve work, lunch at work, or the commute to and from work. Of the remaining 5 hours, 3 are devoted to utilitarian activities in the kitchen and bathroom. This leaves 2 hours for the nurture of any dimension besides work -- for example, recreation. Unfortunately, these 2 hours come at the end of the day, when you and those near to you are tired and thinking of bed. Most young children are already in bed. No wonder corporate America lives for the weekend, or professes to do so.

Now is your chance to break into the open field. If you are currently out of work, try this schedule:

7:00 AM - 9:00 AM:	Out of bed, exercise, shower, breakfast, newspaper
9:00 AM - Noon:	Job search from home office
Noon - 2:00 PM:	Lunch at home
2:00 PM - 4:00 PM:	Hobby
4:00 PM - 6:00 PM:	Job search from home office
6:00 PM - 8:00 PM:	Supper
8:00 PM - 9:00 PM:	Special time with children, spouse, or friends
9:00 PM -11:00 PM:	Relax, television, reading, to bed

Kathy's Insights

If you are unemployed, you will be shocked when you find all the ways you can be sidetracked from the job search. There are the "honey-do" chores, overcompensating for the missed recital, school production, sports activity and the like for your children, and the multitude of "to-do" activities you haven't found the time to accomplish – in short, numerous ways to lose sight of your mission at hand: finding a GOOD job. You may be astonished at how you managed to both hold a full time job and fulfill your household and personal responsibilities. Remember, if there is a vacuum, it will be filled by other people's priorities. The schedule we have laid out for you should provide needed structure, accountability and transparency. Follow a regular schedule, and it will make this process manageable - and keep you focused on your #1 priority.

As you may have noticed already, this routine is a "later to bed, later to rise" schedule, with apologies to Ben Franklin. There is no rule that says you have to get up before a certain hour. The main thing to be concerned about is not length of time, but productive time spent in searching for a job. And lack of sleep ruthlessly cuts down on productivity.

Rule # 1, then, is: GET AT LEAST 8 HOURS OF SLEEP PER NIGHT.

Rule # 2 is even simpler: EXERCISE DAILY.

Again, as you may have noticed, "exercise" has been added to the early morning routine. If you don't exercise currently, examine the reasons:

- No time? Remember, you're out of a job (or the job you want).
- Never started? There's no time like the present.
- Too lazy? You need energy for a job search...and exercise is one of the healthiest things you can do.

Although there are a thousand rationalizations for not exercising regularly, there are one or two compelling reasons to do so. Regular exercise improves your health and makes you feel better physically and mentally. Regular exercise can also give you more daily energy than you ever imagined. A book like the ACSM Fitness Book by a writing team from the American College of Sports Medicine (Champaign, Illinois: Leisure Press) can help you get started. If you exercise, you can tell yourself even on your worst days -- when you accomplished nothing from a job search standpoint -- that at least you exercised.

Jim's Story

My reason for not exercising was that it was too cold outside. I went for years jogging regularly during the summer and fall. When winter came, those outside jogs suddenly lost their allure. Who wants to start the day too cold for comfort? During my last job search, I solved my jogging problem by buying a treadmill and setting it up in the basement. Now I can jog in the warmth of my own home.

Morning

If you adopt the suggested routine, or something like it, a critical portion of your day will be the 9:00 AM to Noon block. It is during these three hours that you will accomplish most of your direct job hunting work:

- Preparing a good resume;
- Getting references;
- Talking to headhunters;
- Developing a network;
- Researching and contacting selected companies;
- Telephone interviewing.

Much of the rest of this book is devoted to the above activities. The point here is that your new routine lets you be well-rested, exercised, and alert enough to make the most of this important morning time.

Lunch

If you live alone and you're looking for a job in the immediate area, you might use this time to network at various local restaurants. If you have a family, we suggest that you use this time to "check in" with your spouse and/or children while the job search activities of the day are still unfolding.

By lunchtime on any given day, you will have certain balls in the air: research findings on a targeted employer, a new job opportunity described over the telephone by a headhunter, call-back messages left with secretaries or on phone mail. Lunch is a perfect setting to discuss the state of your juggling act -- its immediate thrills, spills, and assorted problems and prospects -- without getting too profound or emotional about it. Such "midstream" discussion involves your loved ones and gives them a real-time window into your work and challenges.

Jim's Story

During my most recent job search, my wife and I included our two children (ages 8 and 5) in these midday discussions. As they listened around the lunch table and asked occasional questions pertaining to the search, they were able to understand and handle the situation. No matter the situation, your offspring will sense the shift in your schedule. If they are kept out of the loop, they may develop increased anxiety and discomfort. Age-appropriate explanations that include all members of the family are the best way to overcome this challenge and assure that everyone pulls together.

Mid-afternoon

The greatest addition to your new schedule is "creative or hobby time" for yourself. What is a hobby? We define it as something you do for the love of it rather than the money in it. Often hobbies nourish your passions and allow a creative or recreational outlet. If you have a hobby, it might be among the more common categories:

- Golf, tennis, or another sport
- Hunting, fishing, boating
- Hiking, camping, picnicking
- Piano, landscape painting, or another artistic pursuit
- Stamp, coin, or other collecting
- Reading
- Gardening
- Antiques
- Needlepoint, sewing
- Cooking
- Woodworking
- Electronics
- Home design, decorating or repair
- Cars or car repair

If you don't have a hobby, do anything from 2:00 PM to 4:00 PM except look for a job.

Why is all this so important? Because recreation is re-creation. Each day you take time for more than one of your true interests is a day you feed your needs, feed your spirit, and fill yourself up. You must realize that when you stay sharp and maintain your mental agility, this fullness and satisfaction spill over to the job search. The interaction between play and work is poorly understood, but play has been found to enhance work considerably. Sir Cyril Smith, a metallurgist who helped build the first atomic bomb at Los Alamos, once remarked that most significant inventions have come about as the result of play.

Play, creative time, and hobbies are essential and not frivolous activities. As with exercise, your hobby will add to your sense of worth and accomplishment.

Jim's Story

My hobby is creative writing. I used this mid-afternoon time to visit the local library and write fiction at one of the reading carrels. I looked forward to everything about my daily visit to the library: the drive away from home, the usually satisfying time at the carrel, the books and magazines on surrounding shelves, the groups of tiny human beings in the children's reading area.

Sure, you could spend these two hours on the job search, but you'll find that job search productivity is directly proportional to hobby time. You'll also find that these two hours can turn an ordinary day into an amazing day. (And it diverts your attention from staring at the phone and waiting for email!)

Late Afternoon

Chances are you'll be in a pretty good mood after two recreational hours. And when you return home, there's nothing like finding a few emails to cheer you further. In fact, the hours between 4:00 PM and 6:00 PM are the best time to receive telephone call-backs and exchange emails with your contacts at the end of their busy day. Often between 5:00 PM and 6:00 PM you can reach those key decision makers when their administrative staff has left for the day. If no call-backs come, and your own calls are not productive, you can always make some new calls or send emails of your own, or work on other To Do items.

There is another value to this part of the day. You can use this time to continue reflecting on the objectives and status of your search. If your search is at all like most others, it is never too late and highly recommended to make mid-course corrections in direction or emphasis.

Jim's Story

At one point I had decided that my one true goal was to get a mid-level management job in a large corporation. I purposely wanted to avoid the most senior executive positions and the intense politics that often are included in the package of responsibilities. Then came a call from a former business school classmate, introducing the possibility for me to be a part of the Executive Committee at a small start-up company. The late afternoon hours provided me time to incorporate this alternative, as well as other options, into my thinking.

Supper

Supper can be a good time to plan future events with family and friends, or to learn what your loved ones did during the day. You might be doing this already. Or, for the sake of constancy, you might want to change nothing about your suppertime routine.

Call-backs, such as returned calls from contacts that live in other time zones, may interrupt supper. If they do, treat them with as much urgency as you would a call at 9:00 AM.

Evening

Try reserving a "special hour" from 8:00 PM to 9:00 PM for putting the children to bed, or calling your parents, or discussing things with your spouse or significant other. This should be a different kind of conversation from the lunchtime update; it might draw from your late afternoon reflections to clarify the state of your thinking about the job search, as well as your emotional response to job search developments.

Jim's Story

In my case, I did not look forward to these conversations, but I did recognize their value to my wife and -- surprise -- to me. These conversations almost never concluded on a triumphant note, but they typically reinforced the fact that we were in this thing together. Through these conversations, we knew that we would eventually overcome the challenge, just as we had done when faced with past problems.

In the two hours before bed, you might not want to change anything about your routine. Many people think of television as a mindless negative; we see it as a mindless positive. We've found ourselves watching various shows in order to ease out of the day. It seems not to matter whether it is a movie or a comedy, biography or epic, a drama or variety show or the Weather Channel. It still is a valuable opportunity to step aside from the rigors of a job search.

Reading can be a pleasure and also a mind opener. If you plan to read at bedtime, include material related to your skills and targeted job content. This will allow you to keep abreast of developments in your field while reserving the daytime for your job search.

After all the foregoing, falling asleep should be no problem. If it is, don't worry about it. The next day, take a nap during "hobby time." Then resume your adopted routine as if nothing had happened.

SUCCESS GAUGE
You have mastered S is for Schedule if:
You have determined your schedule, tried it out, and now use it regularly -- and it is a fit for you and your family.

T IS FOR TOGETHERNESS

As the final step in the first two weeks of your search, consider enlisting help close to home. It should come as no surprise to you that you don't have to go through this alone. Whether the central relationship of your life is with a spouse, parent, child, or other loved one, this person can become involved and add value at every step of the way.

How can a partner add value? The following bullets show examples from the twenty-one steps of the search process as described in this book:

Month One: **REST** & **PREP**
- Serve as a sounding board for your career **R**eflection
- Discuss with you pros and cons of options for **E**ducation
- Help you set up and adhere to a daily **S**chedule
- Draw closer to you and show **T**ogetherness

- Serve as a sounding board for your choice of job type and definition of **P**urpose
- Help review, edit and inquire about facts for your **R**esume drafts
- Help you set up and utilize your **E**quipment
- React to your preliminary selections for **P**ersonal references, or suggest references

Month Two: **SHARE** & **HUNT**
- Increase your **S**ocial Networking contacts and monitor activities
- Join you in **H**ealth related activities
- Assist in the identification of **A**ll the People you Know
- Organize the **R**esults Tracking and ensure that Action Planning gets done
- Practice and improve your business **E**tiquette

- Send cover letters and resumes to **H**eadhunters
- Monitor and help **U**nlock the Want Ads
- Expand your **N**etwork of community contacts
- Help choose **T**argeted companies

MONTH THREE: **FIND**
- Help you research and **F**ocus on a company that sees you as a viable job candidate
- Role play **I**nterviews with you
- Help you plan your **N**egotiation with a prospective employer
- Help complete your **D**ecision matrix.

Just because a task is on the list does not mean it is now a responsibility delegated to your significant other. This is one area in your search where there are specific ways to include your loved one, but it would be a huge demand to turn it all over to one person. Those close to you are likely already managing a full time occupation and adjusting to the issues that are part and parcel of your job search.

Also, the above opportunities for sharing do not mean that your relationship during this period will be a fairy-tale journey through paradise. Hot spots arise specifically out of the search process, and both of you should learn to recognize these points of potential flare-up. For purposes of illustration, let's look at a couple of hot spots as they relate to a job-hunting husband named John and a homemaking wife named Susan.

"John, you're taking over the house."

This hot spot begins with Susan's perception that with John at home now, she is losing control of her domain. When she makes a grocery run, she can no longer count on returning to a neat list of messages on the answering machine. John, in fact, took one or two messages for Susan, made a mental note to tell Susan upon her return, and promptly forgot them. In addition, John ties up the phone for hours at a time. Susan, who already feels somewhat at loose ends due to John's job situation, now sees her own guide wires loosening. A solution needs to be reached, and if Susan and John use their time together at lunch or in the evening to identify the new challenges, they can adopt solutions to each and every obstacle.

"Susan, we can't visit the folks right now."

John feels desperate to get as many irons in the fire as he can. He feels the need to stay by the telephone, particularly with a few call-backs outstanding. Susan wants to break away from her norm and communicate with sympathetic and possibly helpful listeners. This is not John's idea of a good time. The temptation is great for Susan to make a solo visit.

Susan and John should stay physically together through this job search period. They might visit the folks for one long weekend. Those folks deserve to know where things stand, and that Susan and John are standing together.

The kind of anxiety described above appears to us to be normal. It seems that nature sets up an extra, continuing drip of adrenaline in times of big change. The trick is to use the adrenaline to your advantage, to channel energy bursts in positive ways toward the objectives of the job search.

Kathy's Insights

Prepare to face unique challenges and circumstances associated with your search for a new job. You and the members of your support system will likely experience the gamut of emotional highs and lows, so it is essential that you avoid adding additional stress. When I was unexpectedly laid off from a position that I held for less than a year, I was shocked and in one lucid moment requested immediate professional help. I couldn't go home and face my husband with the news that I lost my job. My employer arranged an appointment through their Employee Assistance Program. Before I went home that day, I met with a psychologist who helped me gain composure and a short-term plan of action. It was a gift in the midst of my crisis. In addition, my husband has always stepped up to the challenges of my career transitions, helping me identify an appropriate career focus and offering support to see us through to my next career step. You need a support system, and that can include your family, a career coach, your clergy and/or a professional counselor. With enough support you can overcome the job search challenges and find a GOOD job. Follow the process, ask for help, and your transition can bring you closer to your family and take you to new career heights.

SUCCESS GAUGE
You have mastered T is for Togetherness if:
You have enlisted at least one other person who will help you face and overcome the challenges of a job search.

P is for Purpose

Within your chosen career, you must define your basic objective, your top priority, your target for the job search. This does not mean that you have to limit yourself to one type of job and forget all others. Opportunities may arise that are too good to pass up. However, you must be able to answer the question, "What kind of job are you looking for?"

At the beginning of Month One, you reflected on your vocation and went from a variety of possible careers to a preferred career. In this chapter, you will go from a chosen career to a preferred job type within that career. Graphically, the progression looks something like this:

From a selection of job types within your chosen career...

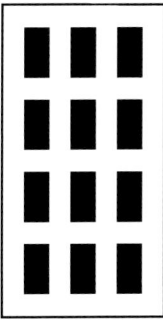

...to a preferred job type:

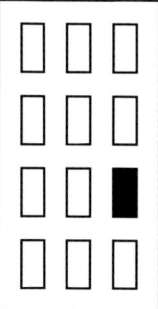

What is a "preferred job type"? In the simplest language, it truly is the kind of job you're looking for. Let's say you are talking to a friend, and you have told her that you want a job in the electronics industry. Then she asks you what kind of electronics job you want to find. If you more or less draw a blank, read this chapter. It will help you formulate a response like this one:

> I want to be part of a large diversified corporation that offers me several structured career paths. I want to manage people on a project basis, which I believe I can do well because of my engineering and supervisory background. First and foremost, though, I want to apply my analytical skills to solve complex technical problems. I'm looking for a salary around $70,000 with minimal travel. I would like to live in the Southwest, but I'll accept anything in the Sunbelt.

That is a preferred job type.

Unlike the Reflection chapter, there is no flowchart to lead you neatly to a conclusion. There are, however, a number of

dimensions which can help you clarify the nature of your preferred job type. These dimensions are as follows:
- Corporate employee vs. consultant
- Large company vs. small company
- Manager vs. individual contributor
- Analytical vs. people-oriented job content
- Over the next three years:
    - Financial need
    - Geographic preference
    - Travel limits
- Next job.

Corporate Employee vs. Consultant

You may have thought at times about going into business for yourself as a consultant. Alternatively, you could join an established consulting firm. Either way, you would find yourself in a challenging and varied job.

As a corporate employee, you would typically be involved in both the design and the implementation of business processes. In this sense, corporate jobs are generally narrower (only one company) yet deeper (design plus implementation) than consulting jobs. Other patterns include: more travel and stylistic freedom in consulting; a bit more money in consulting; and more direct accountability in consulting for sales, profits, and/or utilization of time on work billable to the client.

> **Jim's Story**
>
> When I worked as a consultant for a large firm, I found my job very broad, exposing me to numerous industries and companies across a wide range of business lines. However, my contact with these clients tended to concentrate on program design, with the clients themselves assuming most of the responsibility for post-design implementation. The missing elements for me were not realizing the results of my compensation designs, and not knowing whether the plans in fact motivated employee actions or had a positive impact on the company's bottom line. After six years in consulting, I knew that I wanted a corporate position.

Large Company vs. Small Company

This dimension involves some of the same cultural differences that exist in the corporate vs. consulting dimension: the deliberate, more bureaucratic behemoth vs. the nimbler, more chaotic start-up. An added factor here is solvency in the short run as well as the long run. A large company that looks financially secure today may be tomorrow's buggy whip manufacturer. On the other hand, promising start-ups have been priced out of their markets overnight by the big boys.

Manager vs. Individual Contributor

Some jobs involve the management of people: work direction and monitoring, performance planning and appraisal, staff organization and motivation. These jobs usually require individual work as well as people management; we estimate that the earnings premium for people management tasks at the middle management level is worth anywhere from 15% to 30% of salary. Lower-level managers, including supervisors in production, accounting and other disciplines, spend most of their time managing work crews. Please be aware that not all jobs with the word "manager" in the title manage people. Some managers manage business processes and interfaces across departments; the only people they truly manage are – hopefully – themselves.

Analytical vs. People-oriented

Over and above the actions involved in managing people, some jobs – such as customer service or training – simply involve more people contact than do others. Even where frequent contact is involved, some jobs may require a lot of influencing and/or persuading – as in sales or brand management. At the other end of the spectrum, some jobs require a penchant for analyzing and solving problems. Good examples here are the classic "staff" jobs such as tax, legal, and employee benefits.

Money, Geography and Travel

At the Reflection step, you considered careers in terms of money and other work factors. Here, identifying your preferred job type involves thinking about money, geography and travel in the job you're looking for. This means limiting your time horizon to the next three years or so, or to an interval approximating your expected tenure in the job.

Here are three pieces of advice. Don't sell yourself short in terms of money. You should expect to be paid a fair salary for the position, typically an increase in pay over your former position. Don't overemphasize location to the point of excluding otherwise good matches with your preferred job type. And if you're going to worry about travel, worry not only about overnight travel, but also about long-distance day travel that stretches a normal 10-hour working day into a 5:00 AM to 9:00 PM marathon.

Next Job

Give some thought to the job following the one you will find in your current search. This will help you put your preferred job type in a career context. It can also serve as a reality test to ensure in your own mind that you are on a valid track toward bigger and better things in your preferred career.

Kathy's Insights

The expression "you have to stand for something, or you will fall for anything" comes to mind. Have you ever heard a job seeker say he or she will take any job? This is not a strategic answer. When anyone wants to know what you are seeking, it is your job to make it easy for them to remember you and your goal. When you are specific, it will help your networking contact to remember. If you can, refer to someone who is known to that contact and who is doing something in your area of interest. Your preferred job type, or job objective, is very important for you and for those in your career contact network. You should practice stating your objective to your job search partner (see T is for Togetherness). Those closest to you should also be capable of explaining in simple language the type of position you are seeking. The effectiveness of your search increases with each individual who understands what you are seeking in your next job. Be sure to keep such individuals abreast of your search activities.

Creating Your Job Objective

There are three main content areas of a good job objective:
- the title of the position you are seeking
- the strengths you bring to the position
- your Return On Investment to the employer

Refer to the following Job Objective Worksheet and create your job objective.

SUCCESS GAUGE
You have mastered P is for Purpose if:
You have a clear and easily understood job objective statement that you have shared with those in your network of contacts. Extra points if you have two or more people in your family or support network who can also articulate your job objective.

Job Objective Worksheet

Be prepared to answer the question, "what do you want to do?" Even if this question is never directly asked, you and everyone in your career contact network should use this objective to help uncover opportunities and expand your outreach efforts.

An objective has three specific components:
1. the job you expect to do,
2. your strengths, and
3. the results you expect to produce.

Instructions: Create your objective

1. Identify the job title, i.e. Senior Manager, Administrative Aide, City Manager, Financial Consultant, etc.

    _____

    _____

2. Identify your strengths (especially as they relate to the job you want.)

    _____

    _____

3. Identify the results you expect to produce -- the Return on Investment (ROI) the employer will realize if you are hired. Complete this sentence: "My next employer is going to realize a significant return on their investment in me because I will…." The clearer you are on the benefit you bring to your next organization, the closer you will be to your finding your objective.

    _____

    _____

Jim's Story

My objective would read like this:
I am seeking a Human Resources consulting position where my expertise in designing compensation programs and managing the human capital element will ensure clients receive cutting edge Human Resources solutions to resolve critical organizational challenges.

R is for Resume

Your resume, a summary of your experience and education, will be the main tool in your job search. Imagine a carpenter's hammer, a programmer's computer, an electrician's wire. As essential as these things are to these workers, so your resume is vitally important to you. You will become known first by your resume to most of your contacts, and only later by your words and deeds to a much smaller audience.

You must construct your resume carefully and keep it in mind throughout the search. Also, throughout the search, you will need to make a few refinements. Your resume is a fluid document. It should be revised throughout this process to be targeted for specific opportunities and to incorporate the feedback you will receive along the way. Your resume should be as familiar to you as your name, because at one time or another you will need to explain almost everything in it.

Are you like many job seekers who believe that the main purpose of a resume is to sell themselves? We maintain that the primary objective is to describe yourself, and highlight your accomplishments. Within the descriptive boundaries of your resume, you can then take advantage of many opportunities to sell yourself. The fact remains, however, that a well-constructed resume speaks in large part for itself. By its straightforward presentation of your background, prospective employers can efficiently begin to know who you are.

You may have seen various types of resumes: chronological, functional, targeted, combination and the like. We suggest you use one of three kinds: chronological, chronological, and chronological. This is by the far the most common type for managerial jobs, particularly in the for-profit world, and it provides the quickest thumbnail sketch of the candidate's past.

Jim's Story

The following example of a chronological resume was the one I used during my last job search in 1994. It is followed by an updated resume prepared for me by a professional career coach. The 1994 version was a good resume for me, because it yielded numerous responses from headhunters and targeted employers. I am convinced that three major reasons for its success were its structure, its brevity, and its truthfulness.

JAMES R. STOKELY
9999 Woodland Road, Peoria, Illinois 00999
(123) 456-7890

Experience:

1990 - June 1994   ABC CORPORATION, Peoria, Illinois
$1.7 billion consumer products company.

AVP, Manager of Compensation, Jan. 1994 - June 1994
AVP, Director of Compensation, 1990 - 1994

* As Manager: Assisted the Director of Compensation and Benefits in the planning, design and implementation of compensation programs for 3,000 employees worldwide (payroll: $150 million).

* As Director:
  -- Restructured executive compensation
  -- Overhauled compensation budgeting
  -- Led the development of major management bonus plans and sales incentive designs
  -- Improved the communication of pay programs
  -- Supervised 12 employees
  -- Directed corporate training and development for almost 2 years, revitalizing that department

1984 - 1990   XYZ ASSOCIATES, Raleigh, North Carolina
$200 million human resources consulting firm.

Senior Consultant, 1989 - 1990
Consultant, 1987 - 1989
Senior Associate, 1985 - 1986
Associate, 1984 – 1985

* Provided total compensation architecture, annual and long-term incentive design, salary administration, organization design and performance management to organizations in a wide variety of industries.

* Supervised 4 employees.

Summer 1983	INDEPENDENT PUBLISHING, Tacoma, Washington

Marketing Coordinator

* Planned and implemented publicity, trade and text promotion, advertising, exhibits and special sales for $1 million book publisher.

1978 – 1982	MUSEUM OF SCIENCE & HISTORY, Columbus, Georgia

Director, Adult Education Program

* Planned and administered a $418,000 National Endowment for the Humanities adult education program. Activities included:
  -- 250 events, with 25,000 total attendance
  -- Publishing sales of $70,500 through 1982.
* Supervised 2 full-time, several part-time employees.

1972 - 1978	FREE-LANCE WRITER, Gaffney, South Carolina

* Wrote 4 handbooks, 6 brochures, and various articles for the National Park Service and other clients.
* Wrote and sold weekly book review column to 12 newspapers.

Education:

1988	CERTIFIED PAYROLL & BENEFITS PROFESSIONAL

American Payroll & Benefits Association

1982 - 1984	WESTERN GRADUATE SCHOOL OF BUSINESS

Seattle, Washington

* MBA degree, June 1984. Course concentration in management, marketing, finance.
* Member, Committee for Corporate Responsibility.

1968 - 1972   TEMPLETON UNIVERSITY, Hartford, Connecticut

* BA degree with exceptional distinction in American Studies, June 1972. Course concentration in English, History and the Social Sciences.
* Phi Beta Kappa

1964 - 1968   BRADDOCK ACADEMY, Providence, Rhode Island
* Cum Laude
* Varsity wrestling

Structure

It has been an urban myth for many years that you should only have a one-page resume. There are some people who are best suited with a one-page resume: graduates with little work experience and others with little job movement. Any mid-career person is expected to have a two-page resume.

A worksheet is attached to help you with the basic preparation of a resume. You need to reconstruct the basic timing, places, titles and degrees associated with your experience and education, and then you are more than halfway home. You still must write the thumbnail sketches of what you did in each job. These are best presented in list or single sentence format. For each list or sentence, concentrate on action verbs and pertinent statistics, because employers like to hire doers with a sense for the bottom line. The difference between an okay resume and one that stands out is the inclusion of accomplishment statements. Employers and recruiters can surmise the job responsibilities. Your resume will stand out if you show the WDDIM factor. (WDDIM = What Difference Did I Make, or What Difference Do I Make for present activities.) So from this paragraph forward, you should be making sure that every statement on your resume includes a connection to your WDDIM.

Objective statements are not needed on the resume. You need a job objective, and your resume should support that objective, but saying that you want to work for a great company that will allow you to apply your skills is a waste of attention for the person scanning your resume. Most job objective statements sound good, but they are totally unnecessary on your resume. One technique that is becoming common is to include at the top of your resume an announcement such as:

Seeking a position in:
    MARKETING AND SALES MANAGEMENT
or

Seeking a position as:
    ADMINISTRATIVE ASSISTANT

> **Kathy's Insights**
>
> Every resume writer will be able to improve upon your resume or offer their opinion about various faults. Each writer or resume reviewer will have his or her personal opinion on a given resume's layout, content, length, etc. I have seen resumes that I recently created for clients and can make adjustments to improve the resume, sometimes within a week of finalizing it. What you, the job seeker, must understand is that there isn't a perfect resume – only a good resume which, with input after each use, can be modified for improvement. If you believe your resume is an accurate depiction of your skills, experience and accomplishments and you are proud of your resume, use it. If it is attracting interest of recruiters and hiring managers, you have a good resume. If it isn't gaining interest, explore online venues or the advice of a career coach to critique your resume and gain insight into ways to improve upon your early efforts.

Brevity

Your resume should be like a classical work of art, representing the sculpted and polished product of a talented yet judicious artist. When reading a well-constructed resume, based on forceful verbs and metrics, the reader should want to know more about this or that job activity. In this sense, your resume should "beg the question" through the use of short sentences and phrases. Every experience doesn't need to be fully explained; you will need something to talk about at the interview. Your resume will have done its job if you move forward in a formal hiring process such as having a chance to answer questions over the telephone or in person.

As soon as you put words on paper, the rewriting and refinement process can begin. Send your draft to a trusted friend, share it with your family, and take input from external sources to validate whether your resume is a good reflection of you and your accomplishments. Continue to improve your resume after every interaction with an employer, recruiter or network contact.

> **Jim's Story**
>
> I sent my draft to a recruiter friend, who offered some good suggestions. For example, "a consumer products company with FY93 sales of $1.7 billion" became "$1.7 billion consumer products company." The phrase "compensation programs for approximately 3,000 salaried domestic and international employees" became "compensation programs for 3,000 employees worldwide." Your resume should remind you of a beautiful bush whose healthy growth and deep green leaves are apparent, but whose wild shoots have been pruned. You will constantly be faced with decisions about what to keep in and what to leave out. For example, I dislike seeing a lot of personal traits or experiences in resumes. Having said that, I retained a reference to my high school wrestling over my recruiting friend's recommendation. More than one contact commented favorably on that item. In a previous resume, I alluded to extensive international travel. In the end, you must be a pragmatist: swayed toward what arouses interest, influenced by what works.

Truthfulness

The most successful pragmatists know that truthfulness works. A prospective employer will form an opinion, first and foremost, about your honesty and integrity. If you are in the habit of telling and writing the truth, chances are that this aspect of your character will show through.

> **Kathy's Insights**
>
> Using Wikipedia, a great online tool, I found the definition of a new word; "Truthiness." The word was introduced by the great satirist Stephen Colbert in 2005 to describe things that a person claims to know intuitively or "from the gut" without regard to evidence, logic, intellectual examination, or facts. Do not include truthiness in your resume or your interviews.

In the same way that every bush has bare spots, every truthful resume will show positives and negatives. But how, you ask, will you deal with questions about the negatives? You may have to put some thought into your responses, but this is a lot easier than overcoming a perception of your not being straightforward. You need to understand that the resume must be a fair reflection of you, your accomplishments, career and educational history.

Mid- and late-career job seekers most commonly fear age discrimination. The Age Discrimination in Employment Act of 1967 (ADEA) protects individuals who are 40 years of age or older from employment discrimination based on age. The ADEA's protections apply to both employees and job applicants. But it is a fact that we are a society that values looks, youth and initiative. And yes, there are many jobs you won't get because you appear to have a short runway. Be honest anyway. You only want to work for a company that knows who you are and will give you the opportunity to prove yourself. If you are in the sunset of your career, be open. There are ways to make it difficult for someone to guess how old you are by reviewing your resume, but eventually they will meet you and find out the facts. Your best option is to seek the opportunities most appropriate to your skills with the people who will value your contributions, no matter your age. There is a law against age discrimination, but it would not likely be a productive argument to have with an employer or potential employer.

Jim's Story

My resume shows, besides a number of positives, a clear double negative: a demotion and a termination. I always tried to explain these situations in a way that denigrated neither me nor the company, and sometimes prospects were scared away. On the other hand, several contacts complimented me on my honesty, and I did find a job.

Stand by the truth. For example, I stood by the truth when I rejected an executive recruiter's suggestion to hide the demotion. I also stood by the truth when I referred to varsity wrestling at high school. I knew that my yearbook had made a mistake and had listed only my wrestling for the junior varsity, but I had indeed earned a varsity letter for wrestling in my third year. Even though old classmates might question the conflict between yearbook and resume, I had the truth on my side, and the truth is a good ally to have.

How Your Resume Looks

Finally, a word about your resume's appearance. Virtually all your readers will care about looks only to the extent that the resume makes a generally appealing presentation on the page. This means sufficiently wide margins and enough white space in the text to signal that your resume is easy to read.

Do not use colored paper. In fact, many organizations that take an interest in your resume will electronically scan it into an automatic resume tracking system. Here is an excerpt from a letter sent by the Director of Recruiting at a large health care company:
> To assure accurate scanning into our database, the resume should be "letter quality" and the resume and cover letter should be typed on plain white paper (one side only) mailed unstapled in an 8.5" x 11" envelope (no crease). Please do not use fancy printing or graphics, bold, underlines, italics or small print.

This organization sets a good standard. You need to submit your resume in the format requested and customize your resume for each unique requirement. The basic point, however, remains: the power of your resume will come not from cosmetics, but from fundamental structure, brevity, and truthfulness.

Jim's Story

As I promised earlier in this chapter, here is an updated resume prepared for me by a professional career coach:

JIM STOKELY
9999 Woodland Road, Peoria, Illinois 00999
(123) 456-7890 ~ stokely@goodjob90days.com

Seeking a position as ...
HUMAN RESOURCES BUSINESS PARTNER

World-class change agent with deep understanding of how to bring about significant constructive change in an organization. Successful builder of results-driven teams that deliver economic value. Proven ability to link business strategy with human resources priorities, and to convert priorities into specific action plans. Outstanding record of consistently successful achievement. Works effectively with top leadership. Excellent consensus-building, organizational, and negotiating skills.

AREAS OF EXPERTISE

- Change Management
- Communications
- Compensation & Benefits Design
- Employee Relations
- Employment and Retention
- Headcount Control / Reduction
- HR Strategy Development
- Implementation Planning
- Job Design
- Labor Negotiations
- Organization Development
- Performance Management
- Reorganization
- Team Building
- Training and Development

PROFESSIONAL EXPERIENCE

ABC CORPORATION, Peoria, IL   1990 - 1994
A Fortune 500, $1.7 billion consumer products company.

AVP, Manager of Compensation, Jan. 1994 - June 1994

Reporting to the Director of Compensation and Benefits, designed all compensation plans, and implemented compensation programs for 3,000 employees worldwide.

AVP, Director of Compensation, 1990 – Jan. 1994

Reporting to the top Chief Human Resources Officer, managed corporate-wide compensation programs.
- Restructured executive compensation
- Overhauled compensation budgeting
- Led the initiative to offer a major management bonus plan and targeted sales incentive designs. Presented to and won approval of the Compensation Committee.
- Improved the communication and effectiveness of incentive pay programs
- Supervised 12 employees
- Held double-hat responsibility for Compensation and Corporate Training & Development for 2 years. Overhauled and revitalized the Training & Development function.

XYZ ASSOCIATES, Raleigh, NC   1984 - 1990
A $200 million human resources consulting firm providing compensation services.

Senior Consultant, 1989 - 1990
Consultant, 1987 - 1989
Senior Associate, 1985 - 1986
Associate, 1984 – 1985

- Provided total compensation architecture, annual and long-term incentive design, salary administration, organization design and performance management to organizations in a wide variety of industries.
- Supervised 4 employees.

INDEPENDENT PUBLISHING, Tacoma, WA   Summer 1983
Marketing Coordinator

- Planned and implemented publicity, trade and text promotion, advertising, exhibits and special sales for $1 million book publisher.

MUSEUM OF SCIENCE AND HISTORY, Columbia, South Carolina   1978 – 1982

A 20,000 square foot cultural arts and tourist destination with over 40,000 annual visitors and an annual budget of $250,000.

Director, Adult Education Program

Planned and administered a $418,000 National Endowment for the Humanities adult education program. Activities included the planning of over 250 annual events, with total attendance over 25,000,
- Increased advertising sales by 20% generating new revenue in excess of $70,500 annually.
- Supervised 2 full-time, several part-time employees.

FREE-LANCE WRITER, Gaffney, SC   1972 - 1978
- Wrote 4 handbooks, 6 brochures, and various articles for the National Park Service and other clients.
- Wrote and sold weekly book review column to 12 newspapers.

EDUCATION AND CERTIFICATION

AMERICAN PAYROLL & BENEFITS ASSOCIATION
Certified Payroll & Benefits Professional, 1988

WESTERN GRADUATE SCHOOL OF BUSINESS, Seattle, WA
Masters of Business Administration (MBA) Degree, June 1984.
Course concentration: management, marketing, finance.
Member: Committee for Corporate Responsibility.

TEMPLETON UNIVERSITY, Hartford, CT
Bachelor of Arts Degree, American Studies, June 1972
Course concentration: English, History and the Social Sciences.
Earned exceptional distinction in American Studies
Phi Beta Kappa

BRADDOCK ACADEMY, Providence, RI, June 1968
High School Diploma conferred with Cum Laude Honors
Varsity wrestling

Kathy's Insights

In the updated version of Jim's resume, there are a few new features. His name is Jim, not James R. Stokely. This is a personal preference and will generate opinions from all sides, but my approach is to include information on a resume that is relevant. A middle initial isn't relevant because it doesn't provide content that relates to the position he is seeking. James is his formal name; my advice is to put the name you want to be called at the top of the resume. When you complete the employment application, use your full proper name. Keep in mind that your resume is your marketing tool, not an employment application. As marketing and sales people know, the most relevant facts in an easy-to-read format work best.

Another alteration from Jim's earlier resume version is that the top half of the page includes the title of a targeted position, a summary of strengths, and bullets listing his areas of expertise. This gives the most important facts about Jim first. The bulleted list is a common way to include keywords in your resume, a tool that will optimize the resume's chance of being singled out by web crawlers, spiders and or robots. (Wikipedia: A web crawler – also known as a web spider or web robot – is a program or automated script that browses the World Wide Web in a methodical, automated manner. Other less frequently used names for web crawlers are ants, automatic indexers, bots, and worms.)

SUCCESS GAUGE
You have mastered R is for Resume if:
You have a well prepared resume and believe it meets your two standards:
(1) it is a good representation of you, your accomplishments, career and educational history; and (2) it supports your job objective.

RESUME WRITING WORKSHEET

Note: Use this guide to create a basic resume.

I. **Contact information:** Name, address, phone (one phone number is sufficient, but it should be the one you have the most control over), email address (and if the email name is at all off-color, get a new one.)

II. **Summary of Qualifications:**
   A. Provide the number of years in your current discipline.
   B. Identify three personality traits or words that describe you (detail-oriented, ethical, analytical, flexible, resourceful, creative, results-driven, etc.
   C. Use the following starters to create three sentences that describe or summarize your professional experience:

   Diversified experience in
   Additional leadership experience
   Particularly effective in
   Experienced in
   Specific expertise in
   Trained in
   Knowledgeable about
   Proven effectiveness in
   Demonstrated ability to
   Area of specialized knowledge
   Proven ability in
   Proven success
   Additional experience
   Reputation for

   D. Using details from A, B, and C above, write three to five statements that summarize your area of work, industries and specific talents. Place this below contact information on your resume.

RESUME WRITING WORKSHEET
(continued)

III. Areas of Expertise
    A. List certifications.

    B. Identify special areas of work that you know you are good at, or in which you have a specialty or concentrated work experience.

IV. Professional Experience
    A. List employer (most recent first).

    B. Identify employer's headquarters.

    C. Identify dates of employment, location, and title for each role in that company.

    D. List basic responsibilities.

    E. List one or two accomplishments in each role.

    F. Repeat for all employers or a minimum of 10 years experience. If you choose to show details for the last 10 years, provide summary of earlier experience.

V. Education and Training
    A. Identify the institution name, city, and state.

    B. Identify the degree, certification or diploma earned and your major or course of study and the year of graduation.

    C. If you received any honors, identify GPA (grade point average), scholarships or special designations.

    D. List all training, coursework or seminars that relate to the position you are seeking.

VI. Professional and Community Activities
    A. List memberships, awards, honors, extra-curricular certifications.

    B. Include activities or other personal data that support professional qualifications (for example, Chairman of United Way Campaign that raised over $2 Million, a 22% increase over the prior year).

RESUME WRITING WORKSHEET
(continued)

VII. Personal
  A. Identify hobbies, community service, volunteer work. Note: keep your list of hobbies, community service and volunteer work brief, and include only activities that reflect the skills, leadership and abilities you need for the position you are seeking.
  B. Advise if you are open to relocation, and if so, if you have any target geographic preferences.

E is for Equipment

You can spend the entire 90 days acquiring a full office suite, and you may enjoy focusing on this one thing to avoid all the other difficult parts of finding a new job. But time is of the essence! So follow the guidelines in this chapter, cover the essentials of having the right equipment and methods, and stay organized in order to conquer the job market and find a GOOD job.

You will need a base of operations, and a home office is ideal. It doesn't matter if you commandeer a portion of your finished basement, a ground floor den, or an upstairs guest bedroom. Your home office does not have to be elaborate, nor should it require extensive reshuffling of your home's current order. The most essential requirement is a place to make phone calls, and take phone calls, in privacy.

Distractions will happen if you are conducting your job search from home. You may have a house full of people who will want to pull you into their activities, or others who will provide color commentary on your productivity. Review the S is for Schedule chapter and impress on your family and those who may want to distract you (including yourself) that you must adhere to the schedule to be effective. Be ruthless in establishing your boundaries so that you will be able to carry out your search in a businesslike way.

Jim's Story

Since our computer, printer and answering machine were already in the ground floor guest bedroom, I converted a corner of the room into my home office. This arrangement offered sufficient privacy throughout my job search, with a couple of notable exceptions. In one instance, I had let our five-year old son play a computer game while I made a list of networking contacts. The president of a regional supermarket chain returned my earlier call just as the computer began sounding out a digital version of "Down in the Valley." Very funny. In the second instance, our son was watching cartoons in the adjacent family room when a prominent North Carolina lawyer returned my call. Our son picked up the phone in the family room, realized I was on the phone in the guest bedroom, and left his phone off the hook and unattended. Daffy Duck could be heard clearly over the line. Although our conversation was short, and I was embarrassed the entire time, I was successful in getting the lawyer to agree to review my resume.

Telephone

No piece of equipment will be more important to you than your telephone. Your telephone will be a lifeline to the outside world. Since your search will be targeted and of the sharp shooter variety, you may send out less than one hundred letters, but each one of these letters will be going to a recipient whom you've already engaged in a phone conversation. Letters will be a follow-up tool to telephone conversations. We recommend a dedicated phone line for your job search, one that you have total control over and one that has voicemail. Most people have a cell phone, and it will serve your needs perfectly while you are seeking a GOOD job. Your cell phone should have clear reception; otherwise, you and your callers will be constantly frustrated. Explore alternatives if cell phone reception is an issue.

If you are not in a position to have a dedicated phone line, you need to have a phone available that can accept voice messages. Your outgoing voicemail message should not be recorded by your darling child or children. Anyone calling you to discuss an opportunity should get a short, simple voice message, whether it is on your home phone or cell phone (for example, "this is [your name] and I'm sorry to miss your call. Kindly leave a brief message and your contact information, and I will connect with you at my first opportunity. Thank you.") Remember, your voice message may be the first impression you give your contacts and prospective employers.

Just because the phone rings, you are not required to answer it. Letting your calls go to voice mail has its advantages. When the caller ID doesn't provide a clue to who is on the other end, let it go to voice mail and keep control of the timing and initiation of a conversation. All recruiters are accustomed to leaving voice mail messages. Today, most of us are more prepared to leave a message than actually connecting with the person we call. By not answering the call you won't be caught off guard, and you can review the voice message and prepare to make a return call. Once you identify the person and know that you want to accept their call, you should save the phone number, either call them or answer their subsequent call, and put an end to phone tag.

Jim's Story

One of the surprises of my job search was much higher phone bills for two or three months. Mine averaged $100 to $150 per month higher than normal. One of those bills, for example, included 180 search-related calls. Of these "extra" calls, 140 calls to office assistants, answering machines, fax machines and the like averaged under 2 minutes in duration. The remaining 40 conversations with headhunters, network contacts, and targeted employers averaged 12 minutes in duration. If you rely on a land line, investigate the monthly cost of unlimited domestic calls. If you rely on a cell phone, you may want to upgrade your contract to add allowable minutes.

Computer and Internet

After a telephone, the most important office item you will need is a computer. In the 21st century, you cannot launch an efficient job search without a computer. Although most managers and executives have learned to work with computers to a greater or lesser degree, you may be one of the dwindling minority who remain computer illiterate. Now is the perfect time for you to make great strides forward in your computer skills and employability. One of the main reasons older job seekers are less desirable is the perception that clerical support may be essential to their success. In today's workplace everyone is expected to manage their own correspondence and calendar, and administrative support is not a given with most positions.

Your computer must be capable of accessing the Internet and configured to send and receive email. A standard word processing program such as Microsoft Word is essential for preparing your resume, cover letters, thank you notes and other communications.

When conducting an international job search, consider using a computer-based service such as Yahoo Messenger or Skype for phone calls. These Internet resources matched with a head set will allow you to make Voice-over-Internet Protocol (VoIP) phone calls at a fraction of the cost of typical cell or phone lines, and the phone call quality is usually very good. Depending on your telephone calling plan, your need for mobility, and your comfort level with the technology, such a resource can serve as an effective supplement or even alternative to your primary telephone.

If you do not have a computer, you will need to visit your local library or employment office and become familiar with the requirements, hours of operations, and use policies. A home computer would improve your effectiveness, so if you are without one, consider purchasing or borrowing a computer.

Printer

You'll also need a printer to produce your resume and job search letters. Printers are available in many shapes, sizes, degrees of quality -- and at many prices. Hewlett Packard, Canon, and Lexmark make great inkjet printers that sell for less than $100 and will deliver the kind of quality needed to make a favorable impression.

Fax machine

Of all the wonder machines of the late 20th century, the fax machine was one of the most wonderful. Instantaneous transmission of the human voice took place in 1876. Instantaneous transmission of the written word followed about a hundred years later and eliminated days of waiting on the mailman. This can be extremely helpful for a variety of reasons during a 90-day job search, most often when replying to newspaper postings that only offer a fax number. If your computer is Internet-ready, it may also include software that will allow you to transmit faxes as easily as sending a document to your printer.

Files

Without going overboard, you will want to organize your computer files and your hard copy files. For appointments, your choice is on online calendar or your pocket calendar. For computer files, set up a master job search folder with numerous subfolders for your various contacts. For hard copy files, a plastic crate that will accommodate hanging folders is a basic setup. In the next stage of your search, you will be contacting headhunters (executive search recruiters), network contacts, and targeted employers. Keep an alphabetical file by company name and by last name of all your individual contacts. For each file, keep correspondence (including a copy of your cover letter), articles, other printed material, and a log of activities. Having these records will help you stay current and knowledgeable when you follow up.

    For example, in a file labeled "SMITH, MIKE," with "XYZ CORP" underneath the name, you might write:

8/17/09: I called for Mike Smith, left a message on his answering machine.

8/18/09: Smith called. Though he sees no need at XYZ for someone with my background for two months, he'll review my resume for other possibilities in town.

Getting your resume to Mike Smith can be accomplished using the fax or Internet. The old-fashioned approach is a #10 envelope and a stamp. Since time is of the essence, your attempt to obtain the email address is the best approach. Sending your resume via email also allows your contact to forward it to their colleagues.

Finally, it's a good idea to make a TO DO folder, which will include a running list of priority activities and when to do them. Such activities might include calling back an individual on a certain date, scanning the local newspaper listings, or visiting the library for research. You'll find yourself turning to your TO DO folder at the beginning of each morning.

Kathy's Insights

We are all going as green as possible, so emailing your resume via the Internet is good for the planet and will facilitate the sharing of your resume. When you prepare your resume, do not use fancy paper. For paper quality, you are 100% safe with plain white bond. Any hard copy resume will likely be scanned and converted to a pdf (portable document format) file, so stick to basics for paper quality as well as the resume's layout.

SUCCESS GAUGE
You have mastered E is for Equipment if:
You have privacy to make and receive phone calls, you have a computer and Internet connection, you have a businesslike message on your voice mail, you have a functional printer, and you have a filing system that you can easily use to track your job search progress.

P is for Personal References

You need references – people who can and will vouch for you as a professional – because every employer who takes an interest in you as a job candidate will ask you for some. Getting the right references presents both a challenge and an opportunity. We'll discuss the opportunity later, and we'll concentrate for now on the essential challenge: your references need to be friends with weight, as well as your prior managers.

For everyone, there are three frightening parts of that challenge: friends, weight, and prior managers. First, do you really have friends who know your work? Second, can any of these friends carry weight with a prospective employer? Third, what will your prior managers say about you? Let's look at each of these concerns:

- Friends. We define friends in this context not as "best friends" (i.e., the one to several people in your life to whom you would confide your most confidential information and deepest feelings), but as people whom you like to be around and who like to be around you. Over a period of months or years in a job, you can usually sense who these people are.

- Weight. If most of your friends are like our friends, they aren't likely to carry much weight. While remaining sure to choose friends who know your work, let your friends' titles and organizations influence your choice. Employers prefer references at higher organizational levels because they believe they will receive more candid responses. A senior executive in a major company will probably mean more than the owner of a mom-and-pop store. As for titles, Director is better than Manager, Vice President better yet, and something like General Counsel, Chief Financial Officer, or even President is a real coup.

- Prior managers. The knowledge of one fact – that future employers will want to hear from your past managers in the major jobs you've held – should harden your resolve to obey the following rule: Never, NEVER burn your bridges with the person you work for. He or she may be a poor manager, or dislike you, or whatever, but do not tell that person off. Your job search can withstand one or two mixed reviews from prior managers, but it cannot stand any reports of rage or unpredictability.

If you expect a mixed or bad review from somebody, keep in mind that he or she may be reluctant for legal reasons to badmouth you. Even if you have signed a severance agreement limiting your right to take legal action against the company for events prior to the signing, your manager's reference is a post-signing event and is thus fair game. A legal suit may be the furthest thought from your mind, but the manager doesn't know that, and he or she may very well talk with discretion.

When selecting your references (other than prior managers), look for a mix of peers, subordinates, and internal and/or external clients. Telephone each possible reference and ask him or her to serve as a reference for you. During the call, you might remind the person of specific aspects of your favorable working relationship. Most of the people you ask will accept and be flattered; a few may turn you down. Treat the negative responses as fortunate pieces of self-censorship in advance of disastrous feedback to your prospective employer.

When asked for references by a prospective employer or employer's agent, have a prepared list of your best references. If additional references are needed, divulge others as requested. Your list should be on letterhead that matches your resume with a title at the top (Professional References). On the list include the person's name, title, company name (or, if retired, the name of the company from which they retired), an explanation of your relationship (for example, colleague at XYZ Company for 4 years), the contact phone number and email address if available.

Jim's Story

One of my clients at a former employer called me to find out my situation. Opportunistically, I asked him to serve as a reference, and he gladly accepted. During my most recent job search, I gathered 10 references, including 3 prior managers.

In your search for references, be opportunistic. Where, you ask, is the opportunity in all of this? Your references will form the nucleus of your all-important job search network (described in Month Two). When you call to request a friend to serve as a reference, inquire also about his or her corporate contacts, contacts from executive search firms, or other helpful contacts from the local community and elsewhere. This will give you a critical head-start on the main work of the day: cast a net, land a job.

Kathy's Insights

There are always "back door" references. Someone will always know someone at one of your former companies, and the back door reference can be more important than your list of references. This is because the back door reference checker asks someone they trust to share "off the record" information. The purpose of a back door reference is to save time and effort. The recruiter or employer wants to be successful, and this takes more than just finding the perfect candidate. If you have raised any red flags in your resume or communications, the employer or employer's agent will want assurances that you are what you appear to be; they will seek to obtain more information. If you attracted an employer's interest and thought you were moving forward in the search process and then mysteriously lost all contact, a back door reference may have sabotaged you. Unfortunately, there isn't a strategy to overcome a bad back door reference except one: never provide ammunition for a bad reference. You must always be aware that wherever you work, you are noticed by everyone, and it is your responsibility to maintain a professional image and a reputation for adding value to your company.

Reference Timing

If you are currently employed, it is risky to include your current manager on your list of references. You have control over this list and should only provide the names of individuals whom you want to be contacted now. You may advise the employer that you are willing to provide your current supervisor as a reference at a later stage in the hiring process. It is not expected that your current employer would be needed for a reference until you are at the offer stage.

Prepare your References

In addition to knowing how to reach your references, you should prepare the person for the position(s) you are seeking. At minimum, your reference needs your current resume in addition to specific details about the position you are seeking when the time comes for your reference to be called. You will be supporting your job search by keeping your reference in the loop on the progress of your search, and by asking your reference for any feedback following the call.

Here are a few standard inquiries the reference checker will pose to your references, and we recommend that you ensure your reference will have a few specific stories to share illustrating their assessment.
- How do you know one another?
- How long did you work together? What was the reporting relationship(s)? Do you still stay in regular contact now?
- Tell me about [your name.]
- Tell me about [your name's] technical skills (as it relates to the position you are seeking.)
- Tell me about [your name's] people skills.
- What is the most effective way to manage [your name?]
- Tell me about a time [your name] came up against resistance, and how it was handled?
- No one is perfect; can you explain the areas of development that you would recommend for [your name]?
- Has [your name] shared with you the details of this position, and if so, do you think [your name] will be successful in this role?
- What do you see as the future potential for [your name]?
- Is there anything else you would like to add?

Kathy's Insights

Do you need to get letters of reference from your personal references? The answer is <u>yes</u> and <u>no</u>. <u>Yes,</u> throughout your professional career, you should keep a file with your name on it and add to that file all the "atta boy" comments and recognitions you earn. These can be anything from note cards with flowers from your team after a great win, to an email from a customer who appreciated your efforts, to the annual evaluations from your boss – in essence, hard evidence of satisfied coworkers, bosses, customers and direct reports. This file is where you should turn when you start preparing for a career transition. This file is also a spring of inspiration anytime you need a refresher on your value to an organization. And <u>No</u>, you don't need to find your references and ask for a "to whom it may concern" formal reference letter. It isn't appropriate to include your letters of reference with a resume submission, and you will not want to resort to showing reference letters at an interview. Everyone's time is valuable. It takes an effort to prepare a formal reference for someone. The common practice is for your references to be contacted by the prospective employer and then share comments about you.

SUCCESS GAUGE
You have mastered P is for Personal References if:
You have a current professional reference page that you can provide to prospective employers which includes at least one person you reported to, one peer and one direct report. You have additional references that can be provided if needed. You have prepared the people who will provide a professional reference for you about the position(s) you are seeking, and you know that they can provide factual content for the reference checker.

Month Two: SHARE and HUNT

Now you have passed the initial stage of preparing for a GOOD job. You've determined your career objective and established a system to keep the focus on your career change. You have a resume that accurately identifies your accomplishments and the tools to attract the attention of employers. You are ready to actively begin what most people think of when they hear the words "job search": making contact with a variety of friends, acquaintances, former colleagues, referrals, and assorted others who might help you get a job. This variety is generally known as a "network." In the 21st century, job search techniques have entered the online world. There are a variety of activities that may be very new to you. Are you LinkedIn? Can you post your resume online? Are you able to upload a cover letter? The middle month of your 90 days to a GOOD job is the real crux of getting a new job. This month you will be involved in numerous activities geared toward sharing your information and hunting for the right opportunity. During this period, your search will be in its most people-inclusive phase.

Month two is focused on SHARE and HUNT. You will be sharing your resume, producing your "commercial," and developing your networking capabilities. This month is a time for personal and online interactions that will uncover opportunities and lead you to a GOOD job. SHARE is an acronym that includes Social Networking, Health and Happiness, ABC's of the Information Interview, Results Tracking and Action Planning, and Etiquette.

In this step you will learn about online networking, a targeted approach to informal networking, the value of good health and action planning, and a few tips on job search etiquette.

By the sixth week you will embark on the HUNT. HUNT will share facts on dealing with Headhunters, Unlocking the keys to job advertisements in print and online, and the hidden job market that can be uncovered through Networking and identifying Target employers. At this step you will create and activate your career network and also reach out to headhunters and targeted employers.

The great aspect of this career phase is that there is always another contact to make, another company to research, another place to look to cause a specific employer to take a particular interest in you.

Kathy's Insights

Beware of the double-edge sword of searching for a job using the Internet. There are so many resources, so many sites to visit - essentially a plethora of places to search. Monitor the amount of time you spend "surfing the net" because it in itself can become your full time job. If you are surfing more than connecting, you will be wasting precious time and extending your lack of new employment unnecessarily. Your career search is a balanced and methodical approach that will work, so be careful not to overuse the Internet.

S is for Social Networking

Social Networking may be a new "buzz" phrase, but social networking has been part of the human existence since the dawn of time. Simply defined, social networking is a grouping of individuals who share something in common and band together to seek common goals. In the bricks and mortar world, you are probably familiar with the local Chamber of Commerce. This is a networking organization of businesses that join forces to protect and market business on a local, regional or national scale. As far back as the dawn of recorded history along the Nile River and in the Fertile Crescent/Mesopotamia area, the very cradle of civilization, excavators found evidence that merchants and professional people had gathered together to enhance the economic vitality of their area. This banding together to promote business is an early example of social networking.

The Internet has revolutionized social networking, and its impact is evident in the human resources and recruiting world. Many HR professionals, including recruiters, are mining for passive candidates using online networking resources such as Facebook, MySpace, LinkedIn, Jobster, CareerBuilder, Monster and other career-oriented sites. Job seekers can benefit greatly from social networking by finding contacts within targeted companies, by connecting with former colleagues, and by effectively networking using professional relationships to open doors to career opportunities.

Claiming more than 12 million users, LinkedIn has surged to become the single largest business network on the Web. Kay Luo, Director of Corporate Communications at LinkedIn, explains why: "The main reason that companies are using LinkedIn is to find passive job candidates. [Those not actively looking for a job.] Another reason why companies are using LinkedIn is because referrals from their own employees typically have a higher success rate. LinkedIn helps companies leverage the networks of their employees." Ms. Luo reports the site adds new members at 180,000 per week. For you to be successful in your search for a GOOD job, you need to create an online presence where you can showcase your skills and experience.

In addition to LinkedIn, explore ExecuNet, Jobster, Facebook, MySpace, and ExecuNet to determine which site will benefit you. Don't hesitate to have a presence on multiple social networking sites.

- ExecuNet is an online resource that allows members to connect for a monthly fee This site is designed for executives earning $150,000 annually who are seeking jobs , exploring business opportunities, or wanting to discuss business challenges and share solutions.

- Jobster started out as a site for corporations to host private recruiting events. Since 2004 it has experienced double or triple digit growth annually and connects employers with a valuable audience of job seekers.

- Facebook is a social utility that connects people with friends and will help you share information, photos and music with the people in your life. It incorporates ground-breaking technology that gives people the power to share and makes the world more open and connected. Facebook is the fourth most trafficked website on the internet, connecting 120 million active users.

- MySpace is an online community that lets you meet your friends' friends. With a presence on MySpace you can share photos, journals and interests with your growing network of mutual friends. It can be a venue for business people and co-workers interested in networking, but the most common use for MySpace appears to be for friends who want to talk online.

- Craigslist was started in 1995 by Craig Newmark to share a list of San Francisco events. Today this online community offers local classifieds and forums for more than 550 cities in over 50 countries worldwide. It is a unique niche that is community moderated, and largely free. You can find just about anything on Craigslist including jobs, housing, goods, services, romance, local activities, and advice. According to the Craigslist website, more than 2 million new job listings are received each month.

Jim's Story

I am not a natural networker. For me, networking ranks right up there with fundraising as my idea of a useful yet distasteful thing to do. I have networked when forced to, but as with exercise, frequent practice makes it easier and more productive. I seem to do better when I think of it simply as renewing old friendships and possibly making a few new ones.

Kathy's Insights

Your online presence should be professional at all times. Internet data has a very long shelf life; once it is published, it cannot be removed. You are in the driver's seat when decisions are made on what to publish, so being discreet is strongly recommended - your content will be part of your online identity forever. The online profile will often be part of the first impression you make, so never compromise your future with less than proper language, photos and comments. Long before the interviews begin, and certainly by your first day on the job, many people will learn all they can by checking you out online.

SUCCESS GAUGE
You have mastered S is for Social Networking if:
You have established an online presence and utilized social network sites to find former colleagues or others whom you can reach out to and connect with in order to discuss your career ambitions. You are super-successful in Social Networking if a recruiter, former colleague or company tracks you down to discuss a potential GOOD job.

H is for Health and Happiness

In Month Two we are focusing on SHARE and HUNT, and one of the key components to SHARE is your health and happiness. In Month One we discussed a need for a schedule and for involving your family in your search. These two items are essential to both your physical and emotional wellbeing. During Month Two you will need to dig deeper, evaluate your emotional or mental health, and be certain that you have taken all the steps necessary to present a good attitude. Your mental or emotional health and happiness are key to finding a GOOD job in 90 days.

Put yourself in the place of the people you will be networking with and also the recruiters and interviewers you will meet. These people will be integral to your job search, and they will assess your attitude to determine their interest in you as a candidate and their willingness to assist you in finding a GOOD job. What type of candidate will these people be drawn to -- and what type of candidate will repulse? At the risk of oversimplifying, all people are drawn to those who are happy and have an aura of success. You need to be prepared with more than a great resume. You need a good attitude.

Jim's Story

One day I interviewed with a Fortune 50 company. The company was solid, the city was a match, and the position was right up my alley. Sitting across from me was the # 2 man in Human Resources. I felt ready to rock and roll. Then he asked me why I was looking for a job. In response to this simple and quite logical question, I unraveled. I stammered, glanced out the window several times, and rambled on about trust, the ideal employer, what makes a good job, etc. All my other interviews that day went very well, but that one ensured that I did not get the job. Afterward, I constructed a concise and appropriate reason for my job search.

Challenges to a Good Attitude

The last ending
If your most recent position ended in your position being eliminated for whatever reason, it boils down to an involuntary termination. The forced nature of that action may be accompanied by a sharp blow to your psyche. Without a doubt this is a difficult situation to endure and as difficult to resolve. One attempt may be to put a spin on it: for example, "cutbacks were needed and I was the chosen one." This may make you feel better, but if you know deep down that there was *cause* for being "the chosen," you will need to work through this emotional issue. Working through this issue may take discussion with your close advisors, a psychologist, or other trusted source. In every interview you will have, the one question you will have to answer is:
> What was your reason for leaving your last position?
> or
> Why are you considering leaving your current position?

Do not stretch the truth or sidestep this question. Everyone will judge you on your professional motivations, so be sure you provide rationale that will appropriately reflect your actions and decisions. If the last position ended badly, there is only one way to get past it, and that is to get a new job, a GOOD job. To get a good job, you have to explain the last job's ending, so be upfront and humble. Talk this through with your trusted advisors and make sure you can offer a simple explanation. And practice delivering the answer with a partner.

The length of the Search
As the recession that started in 2007 lingers for many people into the next decade, the length of the search is prolonged and can impact your attitude. The longer you are away from the work that helped define you, the tougher you may find it is to believe in yourself and present a good attitude. Ideally, your search should take no more than 90 days. If it takes more, a new plan is needed. Remember that most people who change jobs report learning that "finding a good job is a full time job." Keep your confident and competent attitude by keeping your job search short and staying involved in professional activities. When the time period of being out of work stretches beyond 60 days, it is imperative that you stay involved in your profession. Seek opportunities for project work, volunteer with your professional association, or seek speaking engagements or writing assignments. Substitute these as necessary for the hobby time in your schedule. If your professional skills erode during your hunt for a new job, you will be a less desirable candidate -- and that will lead to rejections that may ultimately impact your attitude.

Lack of support or misguided support
Your level of support will be reflected in your attitude and your appearance. It is very important to be pulled together emotionally as well as professionally. You must believe in yourself, and your informal support network must also believe in you and can help to keep your confidence up. Believe in yourself and have the confidence to believe in your success in the position you are seeking. It is essential that you have a support system. Those who comprise that system need to provide ongoing support and validation as you go through the process of finding a GOOD job. Misguided support often comes from people who really, really love you but are clueless as to your professional capabilities. When someone repeatedly offers suggestions for your career choices that are incongruous with your objective, passions or interest, that person will negatively impact your attitude. We suggest several ways to

overcome a lack of support or misguided support. For a lack of support, reach out. If your friends and family members are not providing support, or you find they are thwarting your efforts, seek external sources such as the local governmental employment center, a career coach, or a psychologist.

Throughout the 90 days you will be in search mode, and you must ensure you are confident in your abilities and the value you can bring to your next employer. Your attitude, mental health and happiness are essential to attracting the interest of peers, employers, recruiters and all those whom you will encounter in your search. Take steps to ensure you stay positive, involved in your profession, and surrounded by people who can help you maintain a healthy attitude.

Kathy's Insights

One of the common beliefs shared by recruiters and hiring managers is that good people can find good jobs in any economy. As an employee seeking a new position you must be considered *"good"* -- not *"damaged goods."* One of my career coaching clients who was out of work was a great guy, a Chief Administrative Officer with skills to offer many organizations. When we worked together he built his confidence and easily was able to share his "commercial" and present his value proposition during an interview. After every session, he went home with a great attitude. Then his misguided support network kicked in and demolished his confidence. Unfortunately, he was facing dire financial troubles as well as a disabled spouse who was demoralizing him regularly. Our sessions were being countermanded by his home situation. He needed to solve some of his "baggage" issues, and when he did, he landed a great job.

SUCCESS GAUGE
You have mastered H is for Health and Happiness if:
Your attitude is upbeat, you have confidence in yourself, and you have a network you trust to provide encouragement and feedback on your job search strategies, tactics and results.

A is for the ABC's of the Information Meeting

When it comes to sharing your availability and interest in finding a new job, you will need to know the ABC's of the Information Meeting. Right now we are in the SHARE step of your search, and the Information Meeting is all about reaching out and gaining advice and new contacts. Earlier in Month Two we introduced you to networking with "Social Networking." This chapter on the Information Meeting is "Networking 101." Advanced networking will be covered very soon in the next step: HUNT.

The purpose of the Information Meeting concept is to gain information, not a job. We will show you an approach that will not cause discomfort on the part of the person you are trying to see. The main objectives in having an Information Meeting are:

- Further your understanding of critical issues, business conditions, practices, changes and trends in specific industries, and
- Identify key leaders in different industries for you to speak with.

First, let's discuss those people you want to have an information meeting with – the ABC's.

A = All the People You Know
B = Brainstormers
C = Connectors

A = All the People You Know
Starting with *All the People You Know* is easy. This group includes people who you already know but who may not be close associates. They may be neighbors, members of your gym, church or political party, a local banker or civic leader or your own accountant, lawyer or insurance agent. Remember in the first month when we discussed Togetherness? This is where your partner can help you identify appropriate individuals for you to contact for an Information Meeting.

The goal of conducting an Information Meeting with people in the *All the People you Know* category is twofold: getting greater exposure for your interest in a new position, and gaining access to contacts of theirs whom you don't already know.

B = Brainstormers
The Brainstormers are the people who were referred to you by *All the People You Know.* These individuals are a resource of information on:
- Problems, needs and developments in their field
- Activities, people and events in their field
- Ideas on your resume, career objective and/or search strategy
- Suggestions of target companies or industries
- Other Brainstormers or Connectors.

C = Connectors
The Connectors are a smaller pool of people who have knowledge of or are in a position to connect you to a GOOD job. They are the ones who can connect you to:
- Opportunities
- Hiring managers
- Temporary assignments
- Recruiters and employment agencies.

How do you conduct an Information Meeting? The best approach is to arrange a 20-minute, face-to-face meeting. Have a strategy for each meeting and ask yourself: what do I need to know? Set your objectives prior to the meeting and

evaluate your success after the meeting. Look for contacts that will:
- Introduce you to leaders in your field
- Introduce you to other contacts
- Suggest companies that you should target
- Recommend successful recruiters or employment agencies
- Provide guidance on your job-search strategy
- Know of specific job openings
- Continue to act as your eyes and ears.

When you approach someone to ask for their time, make the point that you are seeking their advice and insight, not a job. Here are sample questions you may want to pose in an Information Meeting:
- How did you get into this field?
- What are the challenges facing your industry today?
- Who do you consider to be leaders in this industry?
- Who do you know in this field that I might talk with for additional information?
- Tell me about your background and training.
- What does it take to succeed in this field?
- What do you like best about your work?
- What kind of person seems to do best in this sort of work?
- Would you have any suggestions of companies that I might target?
- Can you offer any suggestions on my job search strategy?
- Would you like to review my resume and offer suggestions for improvement?
- In your opinion, how realistic are my goals?
- Would you like me to stay in touch with you regarding my career campaign?
- Can you suggest any other individuals I might speak to?

Here are some helpful tips for the Information Meeting:
- Set the stage prior to the meeting. Clearly identify the purpose of the meeting. If possible, you can offer a service or "quid pro quo" that will be an incentive for the person to meet with you.
- Be prepared. Practice your approach.

- Establish a rapport by asking personal questions. People love to talk about themselves.
- Take notes. Exchange business cards.
- Bring a resume, but only provide it if requested. It is in your best interest to send your resume via email so that when that person has an opportunity to share it, it is easy for that person to email your resume.
- Send a thank you note for the time, information and input on your campaign.
- Keep the contact informed about your progress.

Jim's Story

A year before my job search began, a work colleague and I spent an enjoyable afternoon at the racetrack. In the middle of my job search, he ran into me and suggested we meet. I eagerly agreed and set up a meeting that week. He turned out to be a Connector, because he gave me a headhunter's spec sheet for the job I ended up landing.

The Information Meeting is an excellent tool to help you reach out and gain advice and new contacts. It is a process that every job seeker can follow, and it will allow you to practice your ability to speak comfortably about yourself. Reach out to your ABC's. You will gain insight and additional connections, and you will be on track to find a GOOD job in 90 days.

Kathy's Insights

Have you ever been invited to a meeting by a casual acquaintance and after preliminaries, you learn that the meeting is to solicit your involvement in a network marketing opportunity such as Amway, Arbonne, Herbalife, etc.? The tactic is an ambush. You are caught unaware of the true purpose of the meeting, and you likely regret the loss of your time. Your opinion of the person who foisted this scenario on you has diminished. When setting up an Information Meeting with a career contact, be open about your purpose, and stick to the amount of time you have agreed to take.

A word about network marketing opportunities: when searching for your next career opportunity, there will be network marketing opportunities or multi-level marketing (MLM) options for you to consider. If you are in Sales and want to stay in Sales, MLM may work for you. If you are not in Sales and don't want to be in Sales, it is a distraction to investigate MLM opportunities instead of seeking a GOOD job that is consistent with your career objectives.

SUCCESS GAUGE
You have mastered A is for the ABC'S of the Information Meeting if: you have identified a list of people in the All the People You Know classification, you have conducted several Information Meetings that resulted in referrals to Brainstormers and Connectors, and you have completed Information Meetings with some of those Brainstormers and Connectors.

R is for Results Tracking and Action Planning

If you are working diligently on your search, Month Two is a very busy time. By now you've taken action, and you need to log the results and keep track of the details. This isn't record keeping for the sake of proving you've been active in your search. Tracking results will help identify patterns and allow you to tweak your strategies. This chapter is crucial to landing that GOOD job in 90 days because it will help you be both efficient and effective. To be efficient you must keep track of information you've gathered. To be effective you must analyze your activities and results and create action plans that will help you reach your goal. This chapter discusses two types of documents: contact reports and action plans.

Contact Reports

With every new contact, you must accurately save details of the interaction, including pertinent facts you learned, and create a follow-up timeline where necessary. It is essential to have a system that works for you to keep track of all this information. The idea is to start with your actions and track the results each week. Having access to the details of an exchange at your fingertips allows you to maximize your efficiency and increase your productivity. It also boosts your confidence. Think about *not* keeping track of the details and always hunting for tiny pieces of paper with time-sensitive information. It will drive you mad and impede your progress.

When you are a mess, you will come across as a mess – and no one wants to hire a mess. Ninety days to a GOOD job requires attention to details.

Your system can be a manila file folder for each company/person involved in your campaign, or an electronic system of folders and files, or a spreadsheet. The system you need is the one that will work for you, allowing you quick access to contact information, a method to keep track of appointments, and documentation that will allow you to manage follow-up actions and timing. When you submit your credentials for a position, use a contact report to document the submission and set a timeline for future actions.

One of the best ways to keep on top of the massive amounts of information you will be gathering is to keep notes from your phone interviews, networking contacts, and interviews. Write the notes as soon after the interaction as possible. Keep a running inventory of the dates and details of your interactions. Make notes that will be available to refresh your memory when needed, including:
- Logistics: date, time, contact method
- Information about the person (i.e. interests and background)
- Problems, priorities, trends in company or industry
- Referrals
- Action plan going forward, including any agreement on future actions

Action Plans

Your record-keeping system is the mechanism you will use to track your progress. We also recommend that you actually write a weekly plan of action. The weekly plan is a simple and concise outline that identifies the amount of time (estimated number of hours) and the activities you plan to devote to your search over the next week. Put it on your computer or write it on a piece of paper at the beginning of the week. Determine your objectives – i.e., where and how you will devote your efforts to market yourself. Identify the activities that will contribute to the achievement of your goals. Throughout the week, record your results. At the end of each week, review the week's plan and evaluate your success.

After several weeks of use, look at your records and decipher which activities are yielding the greatest results. This self-management will boost your confidence and help you stay focused. You will find that confidence is helping you project yourself positively in discussions with others.

Don't overlook the daily framework from Month One – "S is for Schedule" – and if necessary scale back the lunch hour to devote more time to reaching your weekly goals. Each morning, review your weekly action plan and determine a specific plan of action for that day. Be specific and identify the results you want as well as planned actions to achieve the desired result. Measure your goals, actions and results, and tweak the weekly plan until you accomplish your goals.

Kathy's Insights

With a set schedule and an outline of expected outcomes, you will hold yourself accountable and know that you are making progress. Most of us are creatures of habit and are accustomed to following a schedule. Keeping a standard schedule will also prevent you from being sidetracked by other priorities or the "drama of the day." The action planning objectives must be realistic and measurable.

You will find two report samples following this chapter: one to help you track contacts and positions you are interested in, and the other a sample action planner. Here is a sample action plan for a professional sales person who is attempting to move into pharmaceutical sales:

Networking:
20 total hours: 8 hours online, 12 hours face-to-face.
Objectives: Obtain 3 contacts in the pharmaceutical industry and schedule two face-to-face meetings with pharma sales individuals. Attend the Society of Pharmaceutical Sales

Representatives meeting and make three new contacts who would be open to a future information meeting.

Research:
10 hours online.
Objectives: Find industry publications for pharmaceutical sales representatives and review the latest trends. Check for job listings. Find a second professional organization of pharma reps. Identify key leaders in the field.

Correspondence:
2 hours.
Objectives: Send emails to former colleagues and industry leaders to seek information meetings. Secure two information meetings.

Outreach:
3 hours.
Objectives: Identify recruiters who specialize in pharma sales positions, and websites where my resume can be posted that will attract recruiters for pharma sales positions.

Other Activities:
5 hours.
Objectives: Read e-book on <u>Fearless Presentations.</u>

It is a monumental task to find a GOOD job. Every job seeker who was ever out of work will report that "finding a job is a full time job." It is true, but with accurate contact reports and action planning strategies you will be on track to land that GOOD job in 90 days. For those job seekers still employed, an active job search is similar to working on your MBA. You enjoy fewer weekends and sleep less, because some time has to be carved out to further your ambition of landing a new job.

Use whatever system works for you: hard copy information, manila folders or online storage of your contact reports and weekly action planning. It is only a useful system if you are comfortable using it and you use it regularly.

Jim's Story

I remember a high school underwater swimming competition. One of the tips to help you swim further was to watch the small square tiles fly past at the bottom of the pool. Of course, the psychology of this tip was to make you think you were breaking speed records. Part of the strength of the weekly action plans is that, like the swimming pool tiles, they break down a major task into bite-size chunks. I made it a point to track progress against weekly action plans, and this made my challenge of finding a GOOD job a lot more manageable.

Kathy's Insights

Keeping organized records is a useful tool and will allow you to make course corrections along the way. You can streamline your search by determining which strategies are yielding results. Your significant partner/support person can help in this area by assisting in the record keeping. It is not necessary to go overboard with record keeping. The focus must remain on job search activities, not the record keeping of those activities. Certain expenditures in your job search are deductible on your federal taxes, and if you itemize your filing, keep receipts so you can track eligible expenses.

SUCCESS GAUGE
You have mastered R is for Results Tracking and Action Planning if:
You have a system of keeping contact information and a weekly action plan that allows you to schedule and monitor your activities, evaluate your progress, and revise strategies to help you reach your goals.

CONTACT REPORT

Position _____

Name	Title	Company	Address	Phone/Email

Contact Date	Action	Discussion/Information Gathered

Follow-up Plan	To Do By Date	Date Completed

ACTION PLANNING FOR THE WEEK of_____

	Time	Objectives	Activities	Results
NETWORKING CONTACTS & MEETINGS				
RESEARCH (Online, want-ads, industry publications)				
CORRESPONDENCE (Thank you letters, follow-up notes, resume submissions)				
OUTREACH (Recruiters, employment agencies)				
OTHER ACTIVITIES				

E is for Etiquette

Business etiquette and business communications are taught as a semester course in many universities around the country. This may be one area where you are confident in your etiquette competency. On the other hand, you may be totally blindsided or unprepared when it comes to this topic. For the polished who practice the art of good manners, this may only be a review. But etiquette is not only the actions that are customary and appropriate; etiquette also includes self-control, awareness of self, and discretion.

Appearance
This is one aspect of the job search that is totally in the hands of the job seeker. To land the GOOD job you are seeking, you must be genuine throughout the entire process. For each opportunity you have to be in front of future coworkers, managers and company leaders, and you should look the part. Even if the company has casual Friday and that is the day you interview, you should not dress casually; you should dress to assume the job. (If you have been instructed not to wear a suit, you can leave the tie at home.) Being genuine includes your choice of hairstyle, the outfit you select, and the quantity of accessories and perfume. Piercings and tattoos may constitute your genuine persona, but for executive positions, we recommended that these markings not be visible until you are on a more personal basis. There is tremendous bias in the area of appearances, so all job seekers must do some

homework and preparation. Your hairstyle should not be a distraction for any reason. Most interviewers will only notice your hair if it is very dirty. Wear none, or only a minimum, of the following: make-up, nail polish, jewelry. Perfume or cologne is a BIG no-no. Too many people today find smells offensive, even the $100 per ounce smells. For all executive positions a suit is a must for a man or a woman. The rule of thumb is to dress conservatively. Your suit should fit properly, and your shoes must be clean and polished. Ladies, a pocketbook should be smaller than your carry-on bag. And cleavage is not acceptable in business circles, unless the business is an adult entertainment club. You must stand apart from other qualified candidates. If you pay attention to your appearance, you will make a positive first impression and hopefully a good lasting impression.

Handshakes

Practice. Follow the Goldilocks principle: not too weak, not too firm – just right. Ask someone to shake your hand and give you feedback. It is a simple gesture that must be comfortable and genuine for you to give as well as receive. A good handshake lasts for one shake and the accompanying eye contact. That's all it is. Everyone can do it.

Telephone Etiquette

This topic could fill volumes. Recruiters need two things from you: first, a way to leave you a message, and second, your voice at the other end of the phone at the time designated to speak. We touched on the topic of telephone communications earlier, when we offered the suggestion *not* to answer a telephone just because it rings. That concept is about being prepared to speak and selecting the time and place for your career-changing conversations. When you are actually on the phone, telephone manners are important. Ensure you have an appropriate message on your answering device. Even if your sense of humor is appreciated by your friends, any wasted time on an answering device is lost time for a recruiter or for anyone attempting to reach you concerning your career. Plan ahead when you return a call, and determine the information you want to share in addition to your requests. If you get an answering machine, leave specific details about the best time and phone number to reach you. You may also leave your email address.

Never interrupt a phone conversation with someone about your career in order to answer a call waiting. It is rude and sends the message that the next call might be more important than the ongoing call. It also will derail the conversation, and the focus will be lost for both parties. If you are prepared for the conversation, you will not want to be interrupted.

For the same reasons, cell phones should neither be heard nor responded to during any interactions concerning your search. Your cell phone must not sound during interviews, conference presentations, facility tours or a phone interview on a different line. Remember: etiquette is about control and self-awareness. Maintain awareness of your cell phone settings.

Kathy's Insights

It goes without saying, really, to turn off the cell phone - right? No, it really needs to be said – especially for senior executives. One of my candidates, a talented guy we considered "the one," was in the client's corporate headquarters for a day of interviews. His wife tagged along to spend the day in the city and keep him company on the 200+ mile trip. The wife completed her rounds and returned to the office building around noon and called her husband. And he answered the phone while speaking to a member of the senior executive team. That is when he lost the job. End of story. His behavior was interpreted as poor judgment. It wasn't even a necessary call; she was just checking in!

Food & Drinks
There is quicksand in the area of food and drinks for executives. As a guest of a potential employer, you should partake of the food and beverages offered, except for alcoholic beverages. Save the beer, wine, mixed drinks and champagne for later celebrations. While interviewing, you do not want to act too familiar with the people you are evaluating at the same

time they evaluate you. Beverages with a boost can lead to more familiar behaviors, which are not recommended until after a few weeks on the job. Do not order the most expensive item on the menu. Once a utensil is used, do not place it back on the table. Drinks are typically on your right, and bread and salad on your left. And do not talk with food in your mouth. Here is another great opportunity for someone close to you to assist. Go out to a restaurant or simulate one at home, and get pointers on your table manners.

Communications
Your eyes, ears and hands must carry the load when it comes to communications. The eyes are engaged in eye contact with those to whom you are speaking. Do not underestimate the value of good eye contact. Your ears must listen carefully so that you can process both the verbal and nonverbal cues from your interviewers. The hands are responsible for the follow-up thank you note.

Jim's Story

By now, you may be thinking that Jim has made every mistake known to man. You would not be far wrong. Sitting on a couch across from a head of Human Resources one afternoon, I thought I was making a great impression. I left the interview feeling so good that I began scouting out places to live near the company. A few days later, after not hearing anything, I consulted a mutual friend. He relayed to me the HR head's remark that "Jim seemed to be tired." Tired? My friend's next words explained everything: "He said you were almost lying down on the couch." Aha. Sometimes I slouch. I didn't get the job.

After an interview, you can take another opportunity to set yourself apart from the competition with a thank you note. Your note can be formal and sent via snail mail if you are considering a company with a traditional or formal culture. Or it can be an email message if that is the contact method they used. The note is intended to:

- Thank the person or people you met
- Recap highlights of the conversation
- Report on any follow-up requests or clarify any points
- Reiterate your interest in the position, company and location and your alignment with their needs and expectations.

Body language is another communication method that can help you land that next position. Show your interest with physical responses such as nodding in agreement, or shaking in disbelief. Without being a drama queen or king, you should use body language to help get the point across that you are excited and interested. Slouching while discussing the future would not show your interest, but a smile is always an asset.

Repeated calling to the recruiter, HR department or hiring manager is not recommended. At the end of each interaction, politely ask about the next steps in the process and the expected timeline. Keep track of the timeline, and once the anticipated deadline arrives, a follow-up call is acceptable. If you are *the one*, and you don't hear right away, it may be due to internal issues, preparation of an offer, or the schedule of someone who is integral to the decision to hire you. Keep all searches active until you have signed, accepted and returned an offer. Do not make frequent calls, but don't let yourself fall through the cracks, either.

There are a few ways your communications can sabotage your interview. Using foul language, slang names, derogatory statements towards singled-out entities, and being overly familiar or too "sales-y" are the usual suspects when it comes to inappropriate communications during the interview. Sharing jokes during an interview is not standard operating procedure unless you are seeking the position of comedian.

Job search etiquette isn't too different from everyday etiquette. To land a GOOD job, you must know what you should and should not do consistent with good manners. Your self-awareness and adherence to these principles of etiquette will help you stand out from the crowd.

SUCCESS GAUGE
You have mastered E is for Etiquette if:
You are confident that you have a good hand shake, you maintain good eye contact, you have a thank you note template that you can customize for all circumstances, and you know your table manners are up to par.

H is for Headhunters

A logical place to begin when looking for a job is with the recruiters from executive search firms -- also known as headhunters -- who help employers fill open positions. These firms range from one-person operations to large international organizations with offices in most major cities. Some specialize in particular functions, such as finance or data processing. Others specialize in an industry. A search firm is not bound by geography in this day of the telephone and Internet; it is not unusual for the recruiter to be in one state, and the corporation in another.

The headhunter is basically working for the employer, because it is the employer's future openings that will keep the headhunter in business. As the employer's agent, the executive recruiter performs several significant activities:

- With the input of their client, creates a specification sheet identifying the job's key objectives and responsibilities, as well as necessary and preferred candidate skills, personal characteristics, and background to ensure there is agreement on expectations of the right candidate;
- Promotes the position, company, and location;

- Utilizes and expands a large network of contacts to find suitable candidates for the job; and
- Performs preliminary screens on candidates to present only the most viable to the employer.

The above items describe common functions of a "retained search" recruiter, who typically enters into an exclusive contract with an employer to conduct the search. The employer will pay the recruiter's expenses plus about one-third of the job's first-year compensation. Although the employer is bound to pay whether or not the job is filled, it is obviously in the recruiter's best interest to fill the job with a good candidate.

A second type of headhunter is the "contingency" recruiter, who is also paid about one-third of the job's first-year compensation only if the recruiter introduces the hired candidate to the employer. The contingency recruiter networks as extensively as does the retained search recruiter. It is also in the best interests of the contingency recruiter's reputation to match properly the requirements of a job opening against a candidate's qualifications. The contingency recruiter generally does not conduct exclusive searches; this helps explain why you may hear of an open position from more than one recruiter.

There are pros and cons to your use of headhunters. We will first look at three positives:

Positive # 1: Market advice

Headhunters know the market, because they are constantly in touch with it. If you ask an executive recruiter how the market is, he or she can tell you whether it's hot or cold and how demand is trending for the sectors of interest to you. Don't be satisfied with one answer, however; get as many perspectives as you can.

> **Jim's Story**
>
> At a point when I was targeting a corporate position, recruiters were remarking on the great market demand for consulting positions. I ended up talking with several consultants, and because of these activities, significantly enhanced my networking and refined my job objectives.

Positive # 2: Job hunting advice

More importantly, headhunters can give you good suggestions on how to conduct an effective job search. Executive search consultants are just that, consultants, and they have a wealth of opinions to share. You can ask for advice on the quality of your resume, your current compensation compared to the marketplace, future opportunities they may be expecting, or feedback from your interactions. As with market advice, get as much of it as you can from different sources. Some of it will conflict, but patterns will emerge. Listen and learn, for in this case your teachers fill jobs for a living.

> **Jim's Story**
>
> A former classmate of mine who works for an executive search firm reviewed my resume and streamlined several sections. Another recruiter told me not to sell myself short in the marketplace, and advised me to say that "I can be flexible on compensation" rather than "My salary threshold is X dollars." Yet another reminded me to be succinct and to-the-point when answering questions over the phone.

Positive # 3: Fast track

Most important of all, a headhunter may have just the job for you -- and you may be just the candidate for his or her client.

If a headhunter believes that you may be a good match for the open position, you will find yourself on the front end of an action sequence that could be a fast track to the FIND stage (Month Three) of your search. The usual progression goes like this:

> Step 1. A headhunter, referred to you by one of your references or other contacts, calls you and describes the available position.
>
> Step 2. You email your resume and a cover letter to the headhunter, while the headhunter emails the spec sheet to you.
>
> Step 3. Assuming you both like what you see, the headhunter screens you as a candidate via telephone, video conference, in person or a combination of these methods. A report that is a comprehensive assessment of your qualifications is prepared and shared with the client.
>
> Step 4. Assuming you pass this preliminary screen, the headhunter arranges a telephone interview between you and either the hiring manager or an employment manager from the client.
>
> Step 5. If your answers indicate your knowledge, skills and abilities align with the employer's needs, and through the telephone lines you've presented a positive image, you are invited to visit the employer for a day of interviews. This exercise may be repeated later if the first day goes well.
>
> Step 6. If the on-site interviews yield sufficiently positive feedback, the headhunter's client promptly offers you a job. The sooner the position is accepted and filled by you, the faster the search firm is paid. Their satisfaction is matching a great candidate with their client's needs, and the final payment typically occurs after the candidate starts in the new position.

Remember that just being on this track represents a milestone in your search. A sign of successful PREP work (Month One) is having a headhunter call and describe an available position that may meet your search objectives. If you hadn't done your

PREP work, how would you know whether the job might make sense for you?

When sending along your resume (Step 2 above), a cover letter like the example below gets the job done without trying to share too much information too soon.

Every search for a GOOD job, with or without the help of a headhunter, will progress through Steps 4-6. In Month Three we will further discuss Steps 3, 4, and 5 in "I is for Interview." Step 6 triggers two of the last chapters in this book: "N is for Negotiate," and "D is for Decide."

SAMPLE COVER LETTER TO HEADHUNTER – to be emailed

Dear Mr. / Ms. Headhunter:

Following our telephone conversation earlier today, you will find my updated resume attached. The position you described has caught my attention, and I would like to proceed to the next step following your assessment of my qualifications.

Kindly call or email with an update on your search in the next few days. As we discussed, my search is active, and I am involved in the early stages of exploring several opportunities. Additional information about your opportunity is most welcome, as is your assessment of my potential as a match for your client.

Thank you for your time and interest.

Sincerely,

Your name

A few things about headhunters can present problems for you:

Negative # 1: Limited coverage

Although executive recruiters play an important role in matching open jobs with candidates, they can only handle a portion of the positions that become available. And that's not counting the many open slots that are filled internally. Why the limited market coverage? Many hiring managers rely on their in-house human resources function to fill open jobs. Others can't afford or won't pay the search firm's fee.

The answer to this situation is to contact as many reputable recruiters as you can. How can you do this? First, you should ask your references and other network contacts to refer headhunters to you. When you get a call from a headhunter describing a job that is not a match, send a resume and cover letter anyway. You can use the sample letter shown on the previous page, and insert the following paragraph:

> As we discussed, I am looking for (search objective). I would appreciate any leads you might be able to provide. At (previous employer), my ending compensation was $_____. For a job as (search objective) with the right company, however, compensation is only one factor in my search for a new opportunity, and I can be flexible. Additionally, I am open to new locations and welcome your interest for positions based anywhere in the United States as well as international assignments.

Second, you may have been called by one or more headhunters during your career. You may have taken notes during these calls, and have kept part or all of the following information on file or in your database: headhunter's name, organization, address, phone number, and position available at the time. Now is the time to reestablish contact. When you land your next position, make a point of knowing and speaking to recruiters. Their knowledge of the companies they work with and their professional contacts may be an asset to you in the future. Smart business people benefit by knowing the right people at the right time.

Third, you can make some cold calls to headhunters. The Job Hunter's Sourcebook (edited by Michelle LeCompte, Detroit: Gale Research) can help you get started. The main section of this large volume provides information sources for more than 150 career types. Sources include a list of executive search firms specializing in the field, as well as relevant trade associations, periodicals with want ads, and directories with individual names.

The most extensive listing we have seen of executive search firms -- complete with a description of each firm -- is The Directory of Executive Recruiters, published annually by Kennedy Publications (Fitzwilliam, NH: Kennedy Publications). In this volume, over 2,800 contingency and retainer firms are listed by functional specialty, industry specialty, and geographical location.

Another effective approach is to use LinkedIn to find recruiters. Using the *Advanced Search* feature you can enter the title "executive recruiter" and the zip code where you live or are targeting for your search. Or using the same title, you can enter a company name of any of your target companies and find new contacts. One of the features is a choice to select if the title or company is current, past, or a combination of current and past. The folks who are no longer with your target company may be great sources for an Information Meeting as discussed earlier in Month Two.

Kathy's Insights

Executive recruiters who are external to the corporation(s) they work for are not typically located in the geographic location of their clients. I've been based in Florida conducting searches for clients in Omaha, Seattle, Dallas and Bentonville. When searching for a headhunter, it is best to narrow your search by the headhunter's industry or function specialization and ignore their physical locale.

Negative # 2: Joe who?

Headhunters are busy people. Since much of their business involves networking, they talk to many people during the course of a typical working day. Like any of us, headhunters can forget the specifics of a particular case as the days go by. With more advanced computer systems, recruiters track their interactions in order to share information with colleagues within their own organization, and to ensure they keep current on your career objectives, compensation and credentials.

Jim's Story

Once a California headhunter called me with a job opportunity in the semiconductor industry. The job itself was not a good match, but the headhunter and I had an excellent conversation. I sent her a resume and cover letter, then followed up with a telephone call several weeks later. She didn't remember me, even after I reminded her of our conversation's details. Short of physically taking yourself to each headhunter, which is impractical, not cost-effective, and most unwelcome to recruiters, you should check back with your contacted headhunters every 2 to 4 weeks.

Negative # 3: Fair-weather friend?

Headhunters don't work for you; as you know by now, they are agents for the employers who pay their fees. This means that a headhunter is most interested in you when he or she thinks you may be the best candidate for a current search. Otherwise, that headhunter may be a fair-weather friend.

> **Jim's Story**
>
> A recruiter from one of the large executive search firms called me several times about a position in the utilities industry. Through the period of the search, we interacted regularly with what I considered to be very friendly conversations. However, after that position was filled by another candidate, I couldn't get through to the recruiter, even after leaving multiple messages over several weeks.

Headhunters are like public school teachers in that some of them are very, very good. When you find one of the really good ones, establish a relationship with that person and keep in touch. This includes sharing with that recruiter any candidates you think might fit the search of the hour. Such relationships are good business investments for you; they also represent friendly and ongoing contacts in an increasingly impersonal and transitory world.

> **Kathy's Insights**
>
> One unique difference in working with a headhunter is the intermediary role the headhunter plays. Yes, you may have a fair-weather friend when you are a match for a search, but it also true that the headhunter is your advocate. You can speak in confidence with your recruiter to ensure there is an understanding of your needs and priorities. Although the client is paying the fee, the recruiter must look out for your best interest throughout the process -- and if that doesn't occur, you would likely withdraw from consideration.

SUCCESS GAUGE
You have mastered H is for Headhunter if:
You have several relationships with headhunters who specialize in your industry or field. Extra bonus points if a headhunter has fully interviewed you and has submitted your qualifications for one of their current searches.

U is for Unlocking the Want Ads

If you read the local newspaper at all, your reading sequence may start at Sports, move to Page 1, then to Business and maybe the obits. Or for the feminine population, you may read the Lifestyle section first, then other sections if time permits. The classifieds are typically overlooked in daily reading habits. Many of us almost never look at the want ads. Only in times of transition has this section garnered attention from the masses of unemployed.

Jim's Story

I dread the want ads. Why dread? For a long time I believed that someone else had a "lock" on these jobs: the stranger desperately looking for a low-paying job, the company confidently advertising in a buyer's market, the newspaper happily filling its daily pages. I have since changed my mind. There's nothing like responding to an ad by a major company, which I did, forgetting about it, and then answering a telephone call two weeks later from the head of human resources for that company. This led to an on-site interview the following month.

What then, is the key to unlocking the want ads? The key is proper preparation, which means Reflection and Purpose as described earlier in this book. Knowing your preferred career and job type, you can read the want ads with a clear mind, concentrating only on the one or two ads that have something to say to you.

Basically, the want ads represent good news. Each ad is a sign that a company wants to hire somebody. Ads are too expensive for a company to advertise for hypothetical or future positions. The closer an ad comes to your preferences, the closer you may be to entering the final stage of your search.

You should check the major local newspaper at least weekly. Sunday is a good day, because companies know they will catch most readers with some leisure time that day. You also have additional resources available via the Internet. Local papers are providing their advertisers with both print and electronic postings of their position announcements. The option to subscribe to a local newspaper's website is a great way to have immediate notification of new postings. Often the newspaper also offers job seekers a resume posting service. A current trend is for local newspapers to become affiliated with the major job boards (Monster, Yahoojobs, CareerBuilder, etc.) in a piggyback arrangement that allows job seekers numerous resources while generating advertising revenue for both entities. The job seeker is the beneficiary of this partnership.

If you are looking for work in other metropolitan areas, subscribe to either an electronic or paper version of the local edition of the newspaper for each of your preferred areas. A good local bookstore or newsstand will carry out-of-town newspapers from major metropolitan areas.

In addition to the want ads in the classified section, the newspaper is a wealth of information and resources. Reading the paper will also give you other insights into what's going on in any of your targeted locations. The volume of ads and classification of ads in the Employment section are also bellweathers of the market. If you see a dominance of jobs listed under the government heading or medical heading, is an indication of where jobs can be found. You may not see the job you are qualified for, but you should notice trends and be able to identify target companies from the want ads. (In a later chapter in the HUNT step, we will provide greater insight into Targeted Employers.)

The business section will offer insights into area businesses and issues. It will have a calendar of events and meetings. Your networking opportunities will be broadened when you use these listings to find new audiences. The business section often posts legal notices, lists of new occupational licensees, and announcements of contract awards and permits granted. All this information is useful to the job seeker.

When you see an advertised opportunity that you would like to pursue, respond immediately by sending your resume and a cover letter with exactly the information requested. Most companies will ask for your salary requirement and/or salary history. Some will ask for a job code to facilitate the sorting of resumes. It is difficult to predict your salary requirement with only a five-line job announcement. The best response to a request for salary requirements is: "My requirements are commensurate with the current market, and until I have a better understanding of the scope of the position, it is premature to provide a specific figure. Knowing that _____(Company Name)_____ is a fair employer, I believe your compensation package will be acceptable. Additionally, salary is only one component that contributes to my interest in an opportunity, and I would like to understand more about this position and your company prior to discussing compensation."

Do not ignore want ads in non-newspaper formats. A membership in a trade association can yield your next new position. Many professional associations maintain a job posting service for members and member companies. This is a great way to stay on top of the changes in your profession and to passively seek your next career move.

Online databases of job opportunities are the new mecca for job searching. The leaders in the field are Monster (monster.com), CareerBuilder (careerbuilder.com) and Yahoo's! HotJobs (hotjobs.com). Not as well recognized, but growing in market share, is the new kid on the block: The

Ladders (theladders.com), founded in 2003 by ex-hotjobs.com executive Marc Cenedella. To address the unique job seeking and recruiting requirements of mid to upper level executives, The Ladders carved out the niche of posting jobs with compensation at or above $100,000. A basic membership is free, and scaled membership benefits start at $30.

These major services include tools and advice, providing the career management control to the job seeker. The common objective of all job boards is to collect revenue from advertisers – the companies seeking new employees. Tools for job seekers and employers, recruiters and staffing agencies are often available at no cost. To choose between paid sites and free sites, compare the time it takes to produce results from the services offered on the free sites with those offered by paid sites. Then choose the most effective resource.

Another relative newcomer to the want ads picture is CraigsList, discussed earlier in Social Networking in Month Two. CraigsList is a true hybrid of social networking and job posting.

In the spirit of Togetherness (see Month One), the monitoring of want ads may be an activity which someone can do for you. Put yourself in the position of your spouse, significant other, or another loved one. They may be dying to help you in some way, but don't know how. Want ads are as familiar to them as they are to you. Your significant partner has helped you shape (or at least heard you describe) your preferences for career and job type. Why not let him or her in on the joys and trials of your job search experience? This person is another set of eyes and ears in your job search and should be able to promote your qualifications to all who will listen. Providing your partner with some relevant involvement about your job search can lead to those "aha" moments that will propel you to your GOOD job.

In the final analysis, look upon want ads as "gravy." They should in no way be the meat and potatoes of your job search, but they can help out greatly every now and then. Your core job search – based on Headhunters, Networking, and Targeted Employers – has already begun. Now you can add a peripheral view (through the want ads) while moving on to the very heart of your search: networking.

> **Kathy's Insights**
>
> Beware of scams. According to the FBI, scams are on the increase, and the old adage is true: "If it looks too good to be true, it probably is." Especially at times during your search for a new job, you may be vulnerable, so beware. The "post office is hiring," "get paid to shop," and "work from home" advertisements grab your attention, but must be checked out thoroughly. When you are open to new propositions, the "work from home and earn a gazillion dollars" ads conjure up an idyllic mental picture. The one concrete guide I can offer is that if up-front money is required to secure the "job", be a detective: investigate and judge the true feasibility of success realistically.

SUCCESS GAUGE
You have mastered U is for Unlocking the Want Ads if:
You and your designate are reading the newspaper in your target area on a daily basis and monitoring the Jobs section. You have posted your resume and profile to the website of the newspaper in your target area. You are continuing to stay current on business and professional news through the newspaper and your professional association.

N is for Networking

Networking is perhaps your most powerful weapon in the campaign to find a job. In SHARE, Chapter Eleven was devoted to identifying All the People you Know in order to have information meetings and to develop a network of contacts. In this section, Networking is taken a step further, to communication with people in the business world in order to build a trampoline for your career. This trampoline, which is essentially a web of contacts, can serve you at various career points as a safety net or a catapult. During your job search, it can be both.

Why network? Put simply, you must get the word out. People cannot help you achieve your objective if they are unaware of your situation. As you talk with old classmates, business acquaintances, church friends, or even friends of friends, you are making people aware of your situation and your objective. By getting out the word through networking, you are achieving wider coverage than any headhunter can provide. This is because networking can:

- uncover jobs as they develop, long before they get described on a headhunter's spec sheet;
- lead you to hiring managers who have chosen not to use headhunters; and

- generate word-of-mouth from contacts who take an interest in you.

Kathy's Insights

To succeed in networking, you must reach out to people you don't yet know and ask for their help. It is a hundred times easier to do this if you have experienced these types of networking calls yourself. If over the course of your career you have been approachable and have helped others, it will be easy to reach out and connect with those whom you have helped to start your purposeful networking. If you haven't had this experience in the past, resolve to be a networker and connector from this day forward.

Your personal references already form a core for your network. As you develop a sizable network, most other members will sign on less out of friendship than because of professional courtesy or the possibility of a future business return – including the recognition that you can be part of their network. But who are these network members? Let's look more closely at four categories: professional colleagues, schoolmates, consultants, and other corporate contacts.

Professional colleagues

Your selected career probably has a trade or professional association connected with it. If you know of no such organization, conduct a Google search or look for a directory of associations at your local library. If you know a relevant association, but are not a member, you should investigate membership and attend a meeting while seriously weighing the benefits versus the annual dues.

If your trade or professional association publishes an annual directory of members, you can use this to identify networking contacts. Just being in the directory is a sign of professionalism, because of membership qualifications as well as membership dues. Qualifications vary, but generally require current or past experience in the field. Association members tend to be knowledgeable about the local market. Most can summarize the major businesses, and they can give you a feel for the supply and demand for trade labor in their company and the immediate area. Officers of these organizations are well plugged into the network of members. In addition, part of their official role may well be to facilitate networking and the internal job market.

Jim's Story

While networking at my regional Human Resources chapter, one of the chapter's officers helped me find a job several years ago, and another regional officer referred at least ten headhunters to me in my most recent search. The dues to belong to the national and local chapter were well worth the investment, leading me to my next position.

Schoolmates

Classmates, as well as those who have attended the same graduate school, undergraduate college, or even high school at a different time from you, can be great contacts. There are various ways to identify fellow alumni. You can read the class notes that may arrive periodically in the mail. A more systematic way is to utilize special directories compiled by the class at landmark reunions (for example, the 15th or 25th). For alumni not in your class, you might refer to larger directories published every several years by your college or university. These directories are usually cross-referenced by last name, state or country, and work.

> **Jim's Story**
>
> After 25 years of minimal contact, I called one prep school buddy, and we joked that this must be the "old boy" network at work. He referred me to a key hiring manager in one of my wife's and my preferred cities. The manager did not have a job for me, but led to several more contacts in my network. Remember to utilize each school you have attended. The alumni office of the business school I attended sent me, at no charge, a computer printout of the names, home addresses, and work addresses of my classmates.

Consultants

There seems to be no let-up in corporate usage of consultants, including lawyers and accountants. When corporate managers want to be sure they stay on the right side of the law in an uncertain situation, when they want fresh research or a second opinion, or when they simply need help in coping with a work overload, they may very well rely on outside help.

You, too, can rely on the help of these professionals. Even though they may not be working in your functional area, they will know key executives in the area or in companies you are targeting. You may have friends who are lawyers, accountants, or their consultants. If you do, ask them for the names of colleagues as well as corporate contacts. Or you can ask your business-related schoolmates about the consultants they use.

Kathy's Insights

Don't overlook the vendors with whom you established a relationship in your current or previous positions. These contacts are in and out of businesses just like the one you are working for (or have most recently separated from), and they have a vested interest in your landing a new position. If you already like the product or service of this vendor, you are likely to want that item in your new role, and that is a potential sale for the vendor. They can give you current market information, including personnel changes and new businesses openings. Often, based on their interactions, the vendors have insights into the way decisions are made and the quality of an organization. Vendors can be valuable additions to your network of career contacts.

Corporate contacts

As a group, these currently employed workers are probably your most valuable contacts. They can put you in touch with key people at their own company. They can also extend your network to their friends at other companies. In addition, headhunters will call such workers for referrals to possible candidates like you.

Look everywhere for corporate contacts. A good place to start is with colleagues at your former places of work. Then move on to familiar community institutions:

- members of your church, temple, or other place of worship
- parents of your child's schoolmates or playmates in recreational activities
- fellow volunteers at one or more community service organizations.

These contacts do not need to be close friends, but if they are, so much the better. Even if you barely know their names, most will be happy to listen and respond to your situation.

The Calling Process

Now that you have identified a variety of network contacts, the next step is to contact them. You may run across some of your community contacts in person, but you will be calling the majority by phone. We suggest the following telephone opener:

> This is (Your name), calling from (Your city and state). Jane Smith gave me your name. I am currently (between jobs) (seeking new employment opportunities), and would appreciate it if you could review my resume and refer me to any job opportunities that seem to you to be a match with my qualifications.

Feel free to make appropriate modifications. For example, a fellow alum might require: "I saw your name in the Western Business School Alumni Directory. I am a Western MBA, class of '99." The long last sentence of the opener is designed to present your situation and objective in one breath, before any off-putting questions or awkward pauses. A contact might follow this opener with the logical question: "What are your qualifications?" And the conversation is underway!

Most conversations may end with the contact agreeing to review your resume. Good enough. But you might run across a few contacts who are willing to extend the conversation. They may name other possible contacts, or talk about prospects in the area. Listen well in these cases, and take notes.

Many times, you will have to leave a message on an answering machine or with an office assistant. Just leave your name and number, and say you were referred by (name) or state the connection (we volunteer together, our children are in day care together, etc.) If you don't have a connection, you can offer that this is a networking call and that you would appreciate a return call. If you have not received a call back after a few days, call again.

At any one time, you may have up to a dozen outstanding requests for return calls from your outreach to new contacts. We recommend that you avoid the embarrassing situation of receiving a return call and not remembering the pertinent facts. To ensure that you never find yourself in such a predicament, you can keep by the phone a list of call-backs, with name, organization, source of name, and what you will ask them. This way, you'll be ready when someone calls and says, "This is Jane Bowman. You called me yesterday."

The Mailing Process

The sign of success from an initial networking contact is a request for your resume. You will need a cover letter to accompany the resume, and it should summarize your phone conversation. To receive quick action from your contact, you need to take fast action in following up the call. Send your cover letter and resume as quickly as possible. A sample cover letter is found at the end of this chapter.

You might follow this series of steps when sending out my resume:

- Type a cover letter on your computer
- Print two copies
- Label a file folder with the contact's name and organization
- Address a 9 x 12 envelope by hand
- Put one copy of the cover letter in the file folder
- Put one copy of the cover letter and a copy of your resume in the envelope
- Seal, stamp and mail the envelope.

This is the snail mail version. You can e-mail a cover letter and resume after making sure that your contact is expecting your e-mail – and that you have their correct e-mail address.

SAMPLE COVER LETTER TO NETWORK CONTACT

Use an exact match of your resume heading for your letterhead.

Today's date

Mr. / Ms. Urin Thenetwork
Firm
Street
City / State / Zip

Dear Mr. / Ms. Thenetwork:

Following our telephone conversation earlier today, you will find my updated resume enclosed. As we discussed, your help in referring me to any job opportunities that seem to be a match with my qualifications would be most appreciated.

For example, a   (job objective)   would be a match.

Thank you for your time and help. You will be kept in the loop of my job search; periodically I will reconnect. If ever I can reciprocate, kindly let me know.

Sincerely,
(Your signature)

Enclosure

Jim's Story

Over the course of my search, I sent over 100 mailings and a few faxes to network contacts, headhunters, and targeted employers. Because the HUNT process takes about 30 working days, a successful day will find you mailing three to five envelopes by the end of the afternoon.

Follow-up

Two or three weeks after your mailing, you should make a follow-up call to your contact. We suggest the following telephone opener:

> This is (your name). I sent you my resume (give the exact date if you emailed your resume so it can be easily found, or if you mailed it, give the approximate date it was sent). I wanted to call to check if you had had a chance to review the resume, and if any suggestions of contacts, target companies or specific job opportunities came to mind.

This nudge on your part may be critical. The contact may have received your resume, scanned it, thought of a name or another possibility, and then put the resume aside for "further action" which never occurred. Your call may be just the trigger for your contact to mention the name or available position.

SUCCESS GAUGE
You have mastered N is for Networking if:
You are engaged daily in reaching out to your network of contacts, and that network is providing additional leads of target companies, contacts or specific positions. Extra bonus points for success if one of these networking calls leads to an interview.

T is for Targeted Employers

The last major front in your job search campaign involves specific companies that you believe you would like to work for. Proactively contacting 25 to 50 particular organizations rounds out your search beyond waiting for responses from your network outreach efforts. These targeted companies should be big enough to have the job type that would interest you; they should also match your preferences in terms of geography, industry and culture. You definitely want such companies to know about you and your availability.

By targeting companies in a certain locality, you can take advantage of economies of scale. For example, you can visit a scheduled meeting of the area's trade association chapter. The normal way to do this is to request an invitation from one of your networking contacts who is a member. If you know the dates when you will be in the area, you might arrange visits with several of your targeted companies.

But how do you know if you are a match with the company's culture (i.e., values, beliefs, and ways of doing things)? For that matter, who would you contact at the company? And how would you turn one contact into a genuine dialogue with the employer? The answers to these questions will not suddenly come to you in the early morning hours. Targeting an employer involves:

- researching the company
- identifying a contact at the company
- customizing your oral and written communications for the company

Let's look more closely at each of these activities.

Researching the Company

The Internet and your local library are great resources for research. Use your preferred job type (review the "P is for Purpose" chapter) to define your search criteria for targeted companies in one or more of the following sources:

> Hoover's Handbooks (edited and updated by Gary Hoover et.al., Austin, TX: The Reference Press), which are also available in bookstores and online (Hoovers.com), cover 500 of the top U.S. companies as well as top emerging companies. For each company, one page gives a detailed overview and history of the company, while the next page presents financials, key competitors, and the names and ages of key officers.
>
> Standard and Poor's publishes an annual Register of Corporations, Directors and Executives (New York: McGraw-Hill) in three volumes. Volume One is an alphabetical listing of well over 50,000 U.S. corporations, including address, phone number, top officer names, primary bank / law firm / accounting firm, sales volume, number of employees and major products. Volume Two lists birthdate, education and directorships for over 70,000 executives. Volume Three includes indexes by Standard Industrial Classification (SIC) code, state and major city, and corporate family (for divisions and subsidiaries).
>
> Your local research librarian may have additional resources to recommend, including regional and state directories of companies.

Compact Disclosure, which your library may have on CD-ROM, contains most information which over 12,000 companies must file with the Securities Exchange Commission. This information includes financials, the President's letter, largest stock owners, Board members, and top officer names. You can search for companies by industry or geographical area.

Company websites include a vast amount of information including press releases, annual reports, financial information and, of course, career information. The annual reports are of particular interest as they reveal key leaders, current and forward-looking company focus, financials and general information on the state of the company.

Chambers of Commerce are another effective source to help identify targeted companies in a specific city. Their website or a phone call can result in procurement of a list of the major employers in the area.

It is possible to research the culture of a company. A good article about one of your targeted companies can give you valuable insights into the company's culture and prospects. If you subscribe to one or more of the popular business magazines, you may remember an article written about one of your targeted companies. But even if you do have that good a memory, this is a haphazard way to cover the bases. A more systematic way comprises two activities:

(1) At the library, utilize an index to business magazines, such as ABI / Inform, to search the literature by targeted company name. For example, a search using ABI / Inform might yield 100 "hits" against hundreds of periodicals in the database. You can view a list of citations and abstracts, and from these select full texts as needed.

> **Jim's Story**
>
> While researching target companies, I learned that one of my targets was in the midst of a labor war. That gave me valuable insight to the company's needs, and I was able to include in my cover letter a reference to their labor challenges and thereby attract their interest.

    (2)   Call some of your network contacts who live near the company and ask them about it. If they know something about both you and the company, listen to their advice.

> **Jim's Story**
>
> I called several contacts who lived near, or formerly worked for, a manufacturer of long standing in a regional metropolitan center. To a person, my contacts' message to me was clear: this is not your kind of company.

All this research may seem like a slowdown to you after a lot of time on the phone with headhunters and network contacts. Remember that this is but one stage in the process, that it is temporary, and that it can be one of the most valuable things you do to remain true to your job search objectives. If you absolutely need something additional to do during this stage, try calling back some of your earliest headhunter and network contacts.

Kathy's Insights

As you are working to identify your next employer, this is also a time of great opportunity to think out of the box. Do you have untapped potential waiting for an outlet? Is there one employer you thought you would one day work for? I have thought about working at CNN since the network started in 1983. This is your moment of decision to determine which company you would enjoy working for. Which one will help you realize your professional ambitions?

Identifying Company Contacts

Identifying a contact at a targeted company is easy today. You can:

1. Ask network contacts
2. Utilize officer listings in various research sources
3. Use websites such as LinkedIn.com, Google, and industry-specific or skill-specific sites
4. Ask the local Chamber of Commerce
5. Ask an office assistant at the targeted company

1. Network contacts

This method can yield much more effective results than the others. This is because of the weight that some of your network contacts carry with their friends. For example, if a fellow alum from business school refers you to a hiring manager at one of the companies you are considering, you can call and leave a message that includes the name of the Connector who referred you. Your objective is networking and additional information.

> **Jim's Story**
>
> One of my classmates was employed by the best known computer firm in the world and referred me to a Human Resources person who worked in their Talent Acquisition department. I called and left a message on this hiring manager's answering machine to the effect that my schoolmate Jack had referred me, and that I was calling for networking purposes. This busy individual called me back two days later, said he would be happy to review my resume, and asked me to include his classmate Jack's name in the cover letter. "We get about five or six thousand resumes each week," he said. "Jack's name will signal my secretary to pass your resume on to me."

2. Officer listings

In recent years, more publications have appeared which list names of top executives within companies. We have already discussed <u>Hoover's Handbooks,</u> <u>Standard and Poor's Register</u>, and trade association directories. Most such publications update their names annually, but even at this frequency, some executives retire or are replaced in the interim. Still, it doesn't hurt to call with a name. If that person no longer works at the company, you can ask for the name of his or her replacement.

3. Web sites

Use LinkedIn, Google and other industry-specific or career specific sites to find new contacts. Google the company name and see what details you can gather. The advanced search feature in LinkedIn can help find people within a certain company. Once you have a name, you can call the main number and reach out to these contacts. Industry-specific sites such as "jobsinlogistics.com" or career-specific sites such as "jobsintrucks.com" are also useful for finding targeted employers. Affinity groups are an added dimension to source (for example, Latpro.com, a job board for bi-lingual and Hispanic jobs).

4. Chamber of Commerce

If you already have Chamber of Commerce information about major employers in a metropolitan area, you might call them about selected companies on the list. If your network contacts and research do not produce a name, the Chamber is a great place to inquire.

Jim's Story

I had targeted 10 of the 20 companies on one Chamber list of "Largest Publicly Held Companies." Through my contacts and research, I was able to identify appropriate referrals for 8 out of the 10 companies. I called the Chamber, and an employee in the Business Information section gave me contact names for the remaining two.

---

5. Office assistants

You can always make a "blind call" to a targeted company and ask the person who picks up the phone for a contact. Many times, this person will be a receptionist who may or may not know the organizational structure. If this person does not give you a name, ask for the unit or functional area of interest to you. Then ask the person who next answers for a name.

Customizing your Communications

Your contacts at targeted companies will tend to be in more hiring-oriented positions than your wider network contacts. Because of this, they may be more difficult to catch. You may find yourself talking often with office assistants (e.g., administrative assistants, executive secretaries). These assistants are generally intelligent and astute; our advice is to talk with them as if they were their boss. Be friendly. Remember a name and establish a connection. You may be pleasantly surprised when they refer you to just the right person, or when the boss calls you.

When your targeted company contact comes on the line, introduce yourself as with a network contact, including how you got the person's name. Then ask the person to review your resume and refer you to any job opportunities at the company that seem to be a match with your qualifications. Your contact may ask a probing question or two, such as, "How much do you know about us here at Company X?" Due to your research on the company, you can tell a bit of what you know, ending with, "But I'd like to learn more about your company."

Success here is getting the individual to review your resume, or to refer you to the appropriate hiring manager for your interests. If you are asked to send a resume, you should customize the cover letter to the company. The sample letter at the end of this chapter does a small amount of customization.

In a few cases, you may be sending a resume to someone you have not talked with directly, but to whom you were referred by an office assistant. In these cases, you might open your letter with, "Pat Mason of Brenda Harrigan's office referred me to you."

What outcomes can you expect from these efforts? You should be prepared for the usual "We have nothing now, but we will keep your resume on file" letters from many of your targeted companies. One or two contacts may hold your resume for opportunities they know to be developing in the near term. Another one or two might call back with a current opening that may or may not fit with your objectives. Often, there is no response at all as the company does not have a need for your talents at present.

This might seem to you like a low "hit rate." However, even a targeted company "failure" can become a networking success. Sometimes your targeted company contact will tell you up front that there are no openings at their company, but will go on to suggest other corporate contacts. In this sense, missing the Targeted Company bull's-eye wins a Networking prize – and that's not bad.

SUCCESS GAUGE
You have mastered T is for Targeted Employers if:
You have identified a list of 25-50 target employers, found a contact name within each company to reach out to, and have in fact begun to reach out and ask for information and networking assistance.

SAMPLE COVER LETTER TO TARGETED COMPANY CONTACT

Use letterhead that matches your resume or standard email.

Today's date

Mr. / Ms. Ura Target
Firm
Street
City / State / Zip

Dear Mr. / Ms. Target:

Thank you for your time today and interest in following up. You will find my resume attached. Please don't hesitate to share it with others in your company who may have an interest in my qualifications.

Your help in referring me to any job opportunities at _____(target company)_____ is most appreciated.

For example, a   (job objective)   would be a match.

My interest in working for _____(target company name)_____ is due in part to your great business reputation as a progressive company (or other relevant fact). In addition, you are located in a preferred locality for me [and my family.] We would be most grateful for any assistance you could provide.

Thank you for your time and help.

Sincerely,

Month Three: FIND

The previous step of your search was marked by a constant outflow of energy and materials from your home office: phone calls, cover letters, resumes, emails. This third month – the final step of your job search – triggers itself as you receive income from that outflow. In our context, income means an employer expressing interest in you for a currently available position. When that happens, you have reached the point of beginning to focus from a broad set of maybes to one or more specific opportunities.

Such focus does not mean that you should forget the rest of your network. The SHARE, HUNT and FIND steps will necessarily overlap with each other. You can continue building your network, answering want ads, reaching out for headhunters, and targeting employers even while you prepare for an interview. However, as the weeks go by, you will find your energies moving more toward the end-game of our search process: finding out a company's "inside scoop," interviewing with a group of its managers, negotiating a job package, and deciding among multiple job opportunities.

Welcome, now, to the proof of the pudding: the actual closing phase to finding a GOOD job.

F is for Focus

Now that a particular company has expressed interest in you as a candidate for a specific job opening, you should do three things before you launch yourself into interview situations. These three things are as follows: research the company, give the company priority, and guard against "slow-down." Let's look more closely at each of these.

Research the Company

If the company is not one of your targeted few, you should utilize the research resources described in the last chapter (Targeted Employers). Even if the company happens to be among your target industry or geographic preference, you should dig a little deeper. Put the emphasis here on working your network to identify anyone who has recent inside knowledge of the company. This might include a former employee, the relative of a current employee, a consultant to the company, or a long-term resident of the community where the company does business. Insight from a variety of sources will help you prepare for interviews and make better job decisions.

Kathy's Insights

Really do your research and dig to find out the true facts, not just the hearsay about a company and its location. Many people exclude truly viable opportunities due to inaccurate or outdated information. Many people eliminate whole sections of the country based on prejudices. You need the information from a close and current source. You need your feet on the ground to determine if the research you have gathered is accurate. It is better in this case to give the company or location the benefit of the doubt, and follow through on the process. When you are invited inside, conduct your own assessment. You are in control of your future, and you should not categorically discount any industry, company or location until you have actual interactions to make a proper assessment.

Give the Company Priority

At this stage of the job search, two roads are beginning to diverge. The first road, which looks like a six-lane interstate, carries all sorts of automobiles – from Bentleys to clunkers – representing the companies you are interested in working for. The second road looks like a two-lane scenic highway in the off-season. On it travel a handful of mid-priced cars representing the companies that have expressed an interest in having you work for them. Without losing your way back to the interstate, you need to commit yourself to the care and feeding of each car on this scenic highway. These cars are sightseeing, just like the companies that want to look you over, and you can't afford to let any of them pass you by.

Jim's Story

One morning in my most recent job search, I found myself facing a choice: do I call on a half-dozen prime company targets in my preferred geographic area, or do I put the finishing touches on a mock presentation for an interview with a company not in my preferred locality? The answer was clear. I finished the presentation first, then made the targeted calls. No matter all the possibilities pertaining to what might happen with this or that wonderful company, you must focus on what is happening with this good company right here and now. If the company turns out through research or otherwise not to be the right company for you, withdraw politely before the situation develops any further.

Kathy's Insights

Keep in mind that our metaphoric scenic highway is a two-way street. The people representing the company that is interested in you become invested in a successful outcome. Your key contacts will establish an emotional attachment to you. Be open and honest with any recruiter(s) if there are other companies also interested in you or if you are unsure about moving forward.

Guard Against "Slow-down"

If you are diligent about following the steps in this manual, you've been working hard for the past two months. However, it's been self-paced work, punctuated frequently by phone calls, Internet research, postings and networking. If you are between jobs, it's been perhaps six or eight weeks since you left the hectic office pace.

At this point in the process, you may need to remind yourself to pick up the pace – not so much in terms of networking or targeting companies, but in terms of how you are perceived by the employers interested in you. The fact that your search has paid off, that one or more companies have a job available with you as a candidate may seem to you like the end of a journey. It is not. It is the beginning of the journey with a select group of companies that happens to include your future employer. For interactions with these companies, we suggest that you raise your energy level, quicken your talk, and heighten your sense of urgency to levels that you feel comfortable with. Think of it as building the head of steam you need to drive through the critical step of interviewing.

Kathy's Insights

The longer you are away from your trade, the more diligent you must be to maintain your pace in terms of both volume and level of activities. If you are unemployed longer than three months, find some way to be involved professionally. Volunteer for a project in your field or seek consulting assignments. You will be passed over for others who are currently engaged, using their skills in some capacity. Recruiters are especially unfavorably biased towards unemployed people because their clients (your potential employers) do not want to pay a recruiter's fee to find candidates who would likely be easy to find on their own.

SUCCESS GAUGE
You have mastered F is for Focus if:
You are capable of researching and analyzing information about the companies interested in you, you can stay focused on the highest priority activities such as interview preparation, and you are sure you are working at a pace consistent with today's workplace. Extra points if you have actually investigated a company that has expressed interest in you.

I is for Interview

Back in medieval times, an army used a variety of weapons to storm a castle: arrows, catapults and the like. After these had weakened the defender, platoons were called up to carry or guide the battering ram to the castle gates. If these platoons were successful in ramming through the castle's main entryway, the battle was all but over. In your campaign for a GOOD job, the interview is your battering ram.

We will look at two general types of interviews: telephone, and on-site. Both types are very important. The telephone interview generally serves as a screen for the on-site visit, which is crucial to your success. For each type, you need to <u>prepare</u> adequately and <u>implement</u> effectively.

Telephone Interviews

In month two we discussed telephone etiquette. If you skipped that section, it would behoove you to double back and make sure your telephone etiquette is up to par. There are two basic kinds of telephone interviews, depending on who is interviewing you: external screener (executive recruiter) or internal (company) screener.

It is the headhunter (executive recruiter) who will interview you to decide whether to put you in front of the client. Many headhunters will want to know your background from the time you started college, your current role, and your future aspirations. The interview will result in a written summary for the client identifying your past job satisfactions and frustrations, your current job preferences, and aspects of your general nature that may be of interest. Alternatively, an employee of the company itself may interview you. Typically, this employee is a recruiter from the human resources department. The interview objectives are designed to identify three specifics: can you do the job (evidence of sufficient skills); will you do the job (evidence that you are motivated); and will you be a cultural fit with the company.

A headhunter or internal recruiter will either schedule the telephone interview with you or ask you if this is a good time to talk for 45 minutes or so. In preparation for both kinds of telephone interview, you should review, classify, and understand your own past accomplishments clearly and in detail. You should be able to summarize an accomplishment in one sentence, if that is all that is necessary, or tell the whole story if requested. Stories that are succinctly told and illustrate your accomplishments are memorable and strong evidence supporting your candidacy. Your stories are the initiatives or events where you contributed to a successful outcome. They should be sources of professional pride. Sharing your stories will also provide a natural outlet for you to reveal a bit of emotion, too.

> **Jim's Story**
>
> In one of my telephone interviews with headhunters, I didn't know when to stop. I rambled on about one of my accomplishments, delving into the detail of plan design while my listener was silently deciding that I was not a match for the brief, to-the-point nature of her financial services client. Fortunately, another headhunter sent me a written request for information about my past accomplishments in every job, which forced me to construct short and long accounts of each achievement. When he called a few days later, the phone conversation was a breeze.

What should you do after the call comes and the conversation is underway? You should follow three basic principles. First, tell the truth. Just as you did with your resume, stick to the facts and do not exaggerate. Second, show energy through the pace and modulation of your voice. Standing is recommended throughout the conversation; it keeps you "on your toes" and helps you think fast. Third, don't be afraid to show emotion. Phone listeners love to sense emotion on the other end of the line.

> **Jim's Story**
>
> I will never forget speaking with an internal recruiter from a soft drink company, standing outside the rest rooms at one end of a hotel lobby. I described with passion my experience in boosting the morale of several employees whose confidence had been depleted. That recruiter became my strongest ally in an extended interview process which nearly led to a job offer.

On-site Interviews

Assuming the telephone interview or interviews succeed, you will be contacted about an on-site visit. If the interview is in another city, and you have any control over the scheduling, try to fly in the evening before, get a good night's sleep, and attack the next day's interviews with vigor.

> **Jim's Story**
>
> Remember my couch-slouching across from the head of Human Resources? One reason that process ended without a job offer was bad scheduling. I flew into the headquarters city early in the morning (having set my alarm for 4:30 AM), underwent a full day of interviews, and pretty much slept my way through the last critical interview. I didn't land that job – but I scheduled all future interviews in concert with my circadian rhythm.

Your physical appearance is important to those who interview you, and chances are that your appearance is important to you. Most people have a favorite something, be it suit, shoes, or hair style. Do not be ashamed to devote a moderate amount of attention to such "vanity" items. If it makes you more comfortable and confident at these important events, get it right.

You will disappoint your interviewers if you do not have intelligent questions for them. Accordingly, you should review their company material and generate, ahead of time, your own questions about the job, the company, the industry and the people. These questions will also help you get the information you need to make a decision if you receive a job offer.

Should you make up responses to a list of questions that might be asked? Many job-hunting guides take this kind of question-by-question approach. Our advice is to be well-prepared for questions about your background, but do not try to "guess" questions. You can, however, become more aware of differing interview objectives. As we said before: in order to make a match between their needs and a future employee, the company wants to know three things about you: can you do the job (skills), will you do the job (motivation and initiative), and will you fit in (cultural match.) Let's look briefly at three interview styles that help the company determine if you are a match.

"I Want To Get To Know You."

This is a common interview style, in which the interviewer is trying to get a feeling for who you are and how well you would fit in with the company. Most interviews start with a "tell me about yourself" question. Since your resume has already provided a basis of information, this is your opportunity to provide information that is not on the resume. Share details that reveal your passions and values, especially ones that are consistent with the company's values. For example, a candidate interviewing for a sales position might reveal that they are highly ethical and will not compromise their personal ethics for the company.

Jim's Story

In one such interview, I was asked to describe myself with three adjectives. After I did that, I was asked to describe an actual event that illustrated each of the three words. This type of interview may seem rambling and uneventful to the point of your not being able to remember, afterwards, exactly what went on. The key here is not so much the specific content of the interview as it is the general impressions you make on the interviewer.

Selection Based On Competencies

Some companies use a targeted selection process, through which certain competencies are targeted as critical to the company's future success. In this process, also called behavioral event interviewing, the interviewer looks for evidence of such competencies in your background by asking pointed questions like the following: "Can you tell me about a time in your last job when you had to step outside policy to get something done?" Such a question might be designed to get a handle on your initiative or perseverance. The targeted selection process tends to yield more specific questions than usual, which may explore a particular event in some depth. Other behavioral questions include: "Tell me about a time when you effectively led or participated on a team," and "Have you ever had to persuade a senior management of something that he or she was not inclined to support?"

At times like these, you will be glad you did your homework on your own past accomplishments. You should know enough about your achievements to extract at least one example to illustrate the competency in question.

Jim's Story

When asked in one interview to describe a situation in which I "made a stand," I pulled a favorite scene from my inventory and spoke with feeling. To this day, I can't decide whether I talked too long or not. Particularly with this style of interview, you should be sensitive to getting bogged down in the detail. Try to vary the length of your answers by sprinkling in some single-sentence responses. The interviewer's own responses will give you a read on how long to make the next few answers.

"Real Work" Situation

The employer's idea here is to present the candidate with a problem, project, or presentation approximating situations he or she will encounter on the job. This is an effective method and may reflect a key area of need which the company is presently facing or recently resolved. It allows the manager to observe and evaluate in addition to the normal ask-and-listen routine. It also gives the manager a way to compare several candidates in a controlled setting. This "real work" process turns out to be a two-way street. Not only can the interviewers observe you; you can experience their reactions and other behaviors in a relatively realistic way.

> **Jim's Story**
>
> The mock presentation mentioned in the Focus chapter was an example of this interview style. In my telephone interview, two senior executives asked me to think through my approach to a major project which would be undertaken by the person hired for the position. At my on-site visit, I sat with these two executives and made a half-hour presentation based on five overhead slides. Again, situations like these will make you grateful for the preparatory time you invested.

Most candidates will face a combination of all three interviewing styles for each position they seek. Whatever the interviewing style, you can help your preparation greatly by doing a little role playing with a partner as the interviewer. Besides being good for a few laughs, role playing forces you to think fast in real-time situations.

When you do embark on your on-site visit, you should pay close attention to the following three dimensions: time, information, and perception.

Time

The first rule of business is to be punctual. Your on-site interview is the perfect application of this rule. In fact, showing up early might help you.

> **Jim's Story**
>
> At one corporation, I spent 30 minutes reading its just-published annual report. At another company, I spent 20 minutes in the headquarters lobby perusing museum-type exhibits which explained the company's major business lines. These periods of time helped me get my mind "into" the company just before the first interview.

Another aspect of time has to do with the progress of the day. In a day filled with interviews, it is easy to fall behind schedule. Making up lost time is almost impossible, so you must shoulder part of the responsibility for staying on track. The least risky way to do this is to agree at the beginning of the interview when the session will end, then remind the interviewer just before the scheduled end. Your reminder might go something like this: "I'm scheduled to be with Frank Davis in five minutes, but I wanted to ask you this last question...."

Kathy's Insights

Keep an energy bar with you, and when you have a break from interviewers, enjoy it. You must keep your strength at *Full*, because often the last interview of the day is with the senior-most decision-maker. The pace of your day and the volume of information may be overwhelming and energizing at the same time. A reserve of energy is another tool in your arsenal to land a GOOD job.

Information

Remember to ask questions in your interviews. This shows your curiosity and interest, and the answers may very well mean the difference between a good decision on your part and a bad one. Interview questions can yield valuable information about a company's culture: its values, beliefs, and ways of doing business. Sample questions include:

- If you had to describe the culture of the company in three or four words, what would they be?
- What's the best way to succeed in this company?
- Does this company care about the way things get done, or is it only the results that count?
- If I am selected for this position, what would be the biggest challenge to my gaining support for some of the ideas or changes we've just discussed?

You should bring a leather-bound or vinyl-bound notepad to your interviews. Take enough notes to help jog your memory of key insights. Besides holding your notes, the notepad will also help you manage any papers you collect during the day. Bring along copies of your resume, too. Although most interviewers will have already reviewed a copy of your resume, you should have several in case someone needs a replacement copy. A last-minute replacement of one of the interviewers on your interview schedule is not unusual, and your preparation will impress the substitute.

Kathy's Insights

Salary and benefits discussions happen along the way during the interview process. We will cover this topic in depth in the next chapter (N is for Negotiation). You should not initiate such discussions with any interviewer except a representative from the human resources department. At this point, you should simply gather information such as the position's salary range and bonus or benefits offered.

Perception

When you were a child in certain situations, you probably felt the need – or heard the need from your parents – to make a good impression. Like it or not, that is the definition of success for each interview. None of us likes to depend so much on the perceptions of others, but perception is what interviews are all about. As you are led from one interview to the next, you should take quick and silent stock of how the day is going in terms of the company's perception of you. This will allow you to make adjustments as needed, while remaining true to your style and substance.

Try to add value while you are on-site. For example, if a marketing executive presents you with a dilemma involving brand management, don't just give an understanding nod or say that it's a complex problem. Give him or her some advice, to the best of your ability.

> **Jim's Story**
>
> When I was visiting a high-technology company, a sales executive asked me about a troubling situation with one of his employees. Over part of the lunch hour, I drafted a one-page letter from him to the employee. I made an instant and powerful friend in that company.

Often companies utilize multiple interviews. You may start with a phone interview, progress to a video interview, followed by an on-site meeting or two and perhaps even a familiarization trip if it is a new location for you . If each interview leads to another, you are on the right track and getting closer to landing a GOOD job.

> **Kathy's Insights**
>
> A note about video interviews. These interviews take place in two distant cities, typically in an office suite with video equipment and a conference table. This interview will not often exceed one hour in duration. The biggest challenge in this type of interview is to come across as energetic, passionate and engaging while sitting alone in a room conversing with a stranger you see on the television screen. The best way to prepare for this type of interview is to set up a video camera, practice and play it back. Wearing something brightly colored (tie or scarf for instance) will help energize the frame. If you sit close to the edge of your seat, you will appear more animated.

At the conclusion of the interviewing day, be sure to express your interest in the company, the position, and working with all the people you've met. Following the interviewing, don't forget to send a thank you note. The follow-up thank you note may be the one way to reinforce your interest in the opportunity and distinguish yourself from the competition. Thank you notes can be sent via email or snail mail either hand-written or printed. Be sure it is legible if hand written, and in any format there should be no spelling errors.

In interviewing there are so many things to look out for, so much pressure on the moment. To be sure, there is some anxiety involved. After all, you're searching for a job that hangs in the balance. But the good news is that the company is searching, too. Having passed you through one or more screens, and having committed funds to your travel, the company has already made favorable decisions about you. At this point in the process, the company is predisposed to like you. The interview is your chance to strengthen that bond.

Kathy's Insights

The interview is not over until you are home. I know one company that has a car service to transport candidates to and from the airport. The driver who most often is behind the wheel is a very good friend of the head of Human Resources. Any conversation with the driver, or overheard by the driver while you are on your cell phone, may get back to the company. Another candidate, after a long day of interviewing, found himself seated in the airplane in front of one of the people who had interviewed him earlier in the day. You can never be sure who is listening to your conversations. To be safe, keep your guard up until you are back in the safety of your own home.

SUCCESS GAUGE
You have mastered I is for Interview if:
You are comfortable speaking about your own past accomplishments clearly and in detail, whether on the phone or in person. You understand it is your responsibility to be prepared for an interview with the appropriate attire, a few questions to ask the interviewer, and the energy to make it through a full day of interviewing. Extra points awarded for having survived an actual cycle of interviews.

N is for Negotiate

Let's assume that your interviews go well for a targeted company, and that they call to offer you a job, with written confirmation to follow. This is a great milestone in your search and will be a psychological boost to your morale. You may be tempted to accept it on the spot, but there are several good reasons not to.

First, you should at least wait for the written offer, which at the time of the phone call may not be fully committed to paper. Second, you should discuss this with your loved ones, even if it seems like a foregone conclusion in your mind. Third, you have just spent months casting a wide net across many different companies. Your search may have entered the final stage with companies other than the one now offering you a job. Are you sure this company is the one for you? Fourth, you may be able to negotiate a better deal. While the next chapter, D is for Decide, looks more closely at the second and third issues, this chapter discusses covers negotiation issues.

Negotiation should be approached as a collaborative and problem-solving exercise. At the appropriate time you will say something like "I'd like to discuss the details further," but you will never use the word "negotiate." Immediately upon hearing the offer, express your sincere interest and appreciation.

Inquire if the offer will be emailed or sent overnight. Indicate that you need some time to review the specifics and discuss everything with your family. Then commit to a timeline when you will reconnect to finalize the details. Higher level positions are often complex offers, and the process can take up to two weeks to resolve. Typically, candidates will take one or two business days to evaluate the offer before reconnecting with the hiring manager.

At the time of an offer the company is also interested in your start date. This is something to be thinking about after your on-site visit. The greater the need for the position to be filled, the more urgent it is for an immediate start date. At this point in the process, you have one foot in the door and the highest level of interest in you as a candidate. This is when you must prepare to negotiate.

Kathy's Insights

We have used the term "hiring manager," who is typically the prospective supervisor rather than a human resources representative or recruiter. Often the HR manager or the recruiter will "make" the offer, but it is the hiring manager who selected you and the person who controls the budget for your position. The key is to find out who has the authority over the final hiring and offer package decisions. If you don't know, ask. Sometimes there will not be any room for exceptions, and if that is true, you will be informed. More often, however, there is always additional money available to get the deal closed.

You might say, "What is there to negotiate? I knew the target salary level from the beginning of our relationship, and I'm definitely not going to jeopardize the offer by asking for a raise before my first day of work. My targeted bonus potential is fixed at 15% of salary. The company's benefits are fixed and look pretty good to me. This is my bird in the hand, and I refuse to let it fly away by grabbing for more."

This is an understandable feeling. Our proposed method of negotiation is fundamentally guided by this feeling, and is therefore a conservative action based on the following concept: your overall cash flow (income minus outgo) should rise a bit, and certainly not fall appreciably, during this transition. Since there's a lot more to a job offer than salary and bonus, you should study all aspects of the package and consider making 1 (one) counteroffer. This counteroffer should be based on one or more specific cash flow negatives in the job offer vs. your current situation. Let's take this advice one step at a time, beginning with the offer package and ending with the counteroffer.

Offer Package

There truly are many aspects to an offer, and you should be able to turn these multiple dimensions to your advantage. The following list outlines a number of usable negotiating points to consider before making a counteroffer:

- **Salary or base salary.** This is the most obvious element of the offer. A company may be less flexible on salary because of a salary range maximum for the job, or because of internal equity issues that arise if your desired salary is higher than the peers to your position. There are two approaches to base salary negotiations. One is to be satisfied with the offer and not negotiate this item. The alternative is to work toward reaching for the highest number mentioned to you in prior conversations. It is in your best interest to attain the best base salary possible because, with bonuses never a guarantee, you must consider that you will have to live on the base salary. Another factor in reaching the highest base salary is that the if there is a bonus, it is a percentage of that base salary. The higher the base, the higher the bonus. If you choose to leave base salary alone and not negotiate, you can request an accelerated review that will lead to an earlier salary increase.

> **Kathy's Insights**
>
> Today there is an abundance of online compensation data for every position. Salary.com is like the Kelley blue book for cars, and you need to do your homework to be informed even before you interview. When asked your compensation expectations, you can report that your research indicates that the average pay for the target position in that geographic location is $XX. Knowing that employers maintain competitive pay practices, you can also indicate that you expect the company to offer compensation within the current market conditions.

- **Annual bonus.** This annual earnings opportunity is generally between 10% and 25% of salary for mid-level managers. Because the size of potential bonus is tied to salary, you may want to leave this one alone, too. However, you can ask about the probability of bonus payout, including the bonus prognosis for this year, or actual bonus payouts over the past several years.

- **Signing bonus.** This is a prime candidate for negotiation. Few employers will offer such a bonus unless they feel the need for it. A recruiter who knows the salary offer is significantly less than the candidate was previously making may offer to make up for the difference with a signing bonus. If you make a strong enough case for not wanting to take a step backward in terms of a benefit cost or a relocation expense, the company may suggest or agree to a one-time cash payment as soon as you begin work.

- **Equity buyout.** More and more companies are granting stock options to many or even most of their employees. A stock option is the right to purchase a share of the company's stock at a fixed price, which is expected to be less than the stock market price by the time the employee can legally exercise that right. The main purpose of stock options is to orient the work force's attention to shareholder value by giving employees a stake in the company's success.

In your current position, you may have stock options which you cannot yet exercise, or even restricted stock grants in which you have not yet vested as an unrestricted owner. If you are in this situation, you should make the company aware of your expectation for some recompense. One possibility is to calculate the amount by which your options are "in the money" (i.e., the amount by which current market price exceeds the fixed exercise price), then discount for the time until exercise.

- **Relocation.** If you have to move, your needs will include the following:
    - --At least one househunting trip for several days
    - --Real estate brokerage fees on the old house
    - --Buying expenses on the new house, including title search, survey, credit report and appraisal
    - --Transportation of goods to the new house
    - --Travel for self and family to the new house.

    If you have to move before your family, additional needs include the following:
    - --Temporary living expenses near work
    - --A couple of visits home.

    Many corporations outsource the relocation function. Whether in-house or outsourced, it is extremely important to understand the limits of the company's relocation benefits. If any of the above items are not provided, ask.

> **Kathy's Insights**
>
> No doubt you have already concluded that relocation is a big deal for you and your family. It is important that you get your feet on the ground in the geographic location where you will be working. When you interview, try to extend your visit to include an area tour and investigate real estate options. One of my clients had interviewed on the phone and at corporate headquarters for a position that was based in the Washington, DC area. Although the offer was generous and one he wanted to accept, he took my advice to get his feet on the ground and had several startling revelations. To buy a home comparable to his current golf course home, he would have to pay more than double. To spend the amount of his current home's value in this area would downgrade his lifestyle to a smaller home in a denser area. The commute would have been horrendous. He turned the job down and was most thankful for my advice.

- **Benefits.** Compare the benefits package of your current or most recent employer with the benefits offered. Look for shortfalls in the offered benefits on the following elements:
  -- Retirement contribution (i.e., 401-K match from the company)
  -- Your cost of medical / dental coverage
  -- Flexible reimbursement account
  -- Life insurance coverage.

  There are other benefits, of course, but you can argue cash flow shortfalls in the above. Your case is stronger if you are currently employed.

- **Perquisites.** If you are currently employed in a company's upper levels, you may be receiving a country club membership, tax return preparation, financial advisory services, free parking, a car or car allowance, supplemental benefits, or other "perks." You can also argue cash flow if any of these is lost.

- **Cost of living.** Some areas of the country cost more to live in than do others. In many cases, higher cost-of-living is due in part to higher cost-of-labor, which should be reflected in your salary offer. Still, cost-of-living indices tend to be higher than cost-of-labor.

  Cost-of-living differences are due to differences in state and local taxes, housing, transportation, utilities, food and other consumables. If you are moving to a new area, compare your future taxes vs. the taxes you are leaving behind. Compare also your current home to the cost of comparable houses in your new location. Your prospective employer should listen to cash flow arguments based on higher taxes or a higher mortgage, and will not want to force you and your family into a significantly lower – and possibly unsatisfactory – lifestyle.

- **Time and timing.** The start date is negotiable as well as vacation time allowance.

Now armed with one or more negotiating points, you should be in a better position to structure a counteroffer.

Counteroffer

Companies like to say they don't bargain with new hires, but our experience is that most will listen to a well-reasoned counteroffer. Support may come from the company's staffing department, which is usually ready to move on to a new hiring assignment after mentally "booking" your coming on board. Internal recruiters, who can have significant influence on the hiring manager, don't like to see a good match get away so late in the game.

Having said this, it must be emphasized that your counteroffer should not make the hiring manager feel party to an ultimatum, or backed into a financial corner. You should not present the manager with a shopping list of items, nor should you make more than one counteroffer. You don't want to earn a reputation as a royal pain before crossing the threshold at your new employer.

> **Jim's Story**
>
> One senior-level manager I know negotiated back and forth on the nickels and dimes of the top marketing job for a professional sports association. He finally blew the whole deal by giving the impression that he was too detail-oriented, too slow to make a decision, and not committed enough to the organization.

Your counteroffer should be gentle in style, but with the hard chiseled substance of an arrowhead. You might convey it verbally, either over the telephone or during a pre-decision visit by you and your spouse. Your presentation might go something like this:

> You know, Frank, this is one of my top two opportunities. I've discussed all the financial ins and outs with my family, and we're looking at about a $10,000 loss in funds once we make the move. The salary and bonus potential are fine, no problems there. And I'd be happy to start two weeks from today as you indicated. But we need an additional house hunting trip and a couple of visits home for me over the next two months. I'm sure you can understand that. I'd also be losing a 401-K match at my former employer of about $3,000. Finally, we'd be picking up 5% to 6% in state and local taxes over and above what we have now. Frank, I'm not asking you for $10,000 more in salary. But what do you think you can do to help us out?

This might very well lead to a signing bonus of $7,000 ($10,000 minus the 401-K match). If you do make a counteroffer, the job should truly be your first or second choice. The company may expect you to say yes immediately after their positive response to the counteroffer, or soon after their negative response. This means that you should have worked through your final job decision to the point of feeling comfortable with a yes or a no. Making that decision is the subject of our next and final step in the process.

Once you have evaluated the variables and pitched your counteroffer, it is time to obtain agreement and request the final offer in writing.

Kathy's Insights

If you are working with an external recruiter, you have already thoroughly discussed the details of your current and expected compensation. This recruiter is responsible to their client to find a candidate within a targeted range. There are circumstances where the employer will go above the targeted range, often when it is a highly specialized position with a small talent pool or if your skills can be applied to a broader role. The recruiter is paid a percentage of your salary (sometimes only the base, other times base plus signing bonus or other combination), and it is in the recruiter's best interest to have you accept the highest possible salary. The recruiter will discuss your expectations early on with their client so there are no surprises. Often, that recruiter is your best ally during the negotiation phase.

SUCCESS GAUGE
You have mastered N is for Negotiation if:
You expressed sincere interest when you received the offer, have completed your analysis of all the variables, and feel comfortable asking for clarification and pitching a counteroffer.

D is for Decide

As our 90-day time period draws to a close, you may be in the fortunate position of having to decide between two – or among more than two – favorable offers. If you are not the only person making this decision (i.e., if you are part of a family), you will almost certainly need some sort of decision-making method above and beyond following your gut. Even if you are making this decision alone, you want to be sure that your excitement about one aspect of the job opportunity is not blinding you to red flags elsewhere.

You may recall that back in the Reflection chapter you were advised to follow your gut when planning a career. Are we being inconsistent now? No. Your emotions can guide the way to a broad field of opportunity, but you may need a method to help point to a specific job opportunity. Emotions remain important; it's just that they are now channeled for finer measurement.

> **Kathy's Insights**
>
> Even if you only have one offer, it is critical to objectively evaluate if this opportunity is right for you, both personally and professionally. Once you break down the key factors and analyze your option, you may realize that you will not have a successful long term future if you accept this offer and decide to continue searching for your GOOD job.

Here is a helpful decision-making method that can help you decide among job opportunities. It is a five step method, as follows:

1. Identify important decision factors
2. Weight each factor
3. Devise a scoring scale, and identify a threshold score for each factor
4. Score a job opportunity against each factor
5. Compare one job opportunity's total scores against another.

Let's look more closely at each of these steps.

Identify Decision Factors

In the Purpose chapter, you identified elements of your preferred job type, including job responsibilities, travel, and pay. This preferred job type is a good place to begin identifying between 6 and 10 factors that are most important to you in making your decision. Here is an example of eight factors that may be considered in making your decision:

1. My boss
2. Job role / job resources / job impact
3. Company products / company vision / company culture
4. Risk of job failure or company failure
5. Pay level
6. Geographic location
7. Future career opportunity
8. Work hours and travel

You can break down additional elements to analyze that are related to the company, the position, the compensation, your personal preferences or the community. It is up to you to identify your priorities, but be sure to approach this assessment with objective criteria in order to make the right decision.

Weight Each Factor

It would be a great coincidence if all of your factors were equally important to you, but that is never the case. You now can assign each factor a weight, but guard against building in too much discrepancy across factors. For example, if the previous list were a prioritized list, with the first factor being most important, the weighting could have been 8 to "My boss," 7 to the "job role", and so on down to 2 for "Future career opportunity" and 1 for "Work hours and travel." However, it would be misleading to rank "My boss" as four times more important than "Career opportunity" (8 divided by 2 equals 4), or 8 times more important than "Work hours and travel". You might end up assigning a weight of 1.5 to the first two factors, 1 to the next five, and 0.5 to the last factor.

Devise a Scale and Identify Threshold Scores

Choose a scale that works for you. A scale of 1 to 5 is broad enough, while a 1-to-3 scale may not discriminate enough for you – and a 1-to-10 scale may be overkill. You may prefer any one of these three, or some other alternative. This is a great time to include your significant other at this critical juncture; ask for assistance with the analysis and scoring.

Next, identify a threshold score for each factor. Here, "threshold" means the lowest score you would accept on a factor before you or your family would have to make significant compromises in work or lifestyle. If a score on a factor for a particular job opportunity is below the factor's threshold, then the total score for that job opportunity should be reduced by 20%. Your threshold scores may be higher for your top-priority factors than they are for the rest. This makes sense, for you are saying, "On the two or three most critical pieces of this puzzle, I won't accept less than a good situation."

Score an Opportunity

Before you score a job opportunity against your factors, you might organize your notes and thoughts about that opportunity. When scoring, take either a conservative, liberal, or middle-of-the-road approach. Remember which approach you took, and do the same when scoring your other job opportunities.

After you assign your "raw score" to each factor for a given job opportunity, multiply each factor's weight by its score to yield a "weighted score." Add these up, deduct 20% for each "raw score" below that factor's threshold, and you have your total.

Using the eight-factor example above, your decision table might look like this:

Job #1

Decision Factor	Threshold	Weight	Raw Score	Weighted Score
Boss	3	1.5	4	6
Role, etc	3	1.5	2	3
Products, etc.	2	1	3	3
Risk	2	1	2	2
Pay	2	1	5	5
Location	2	1	4	4
Career	2	1	3	3
Work hours	1	.5	2	1
SUBTOTAL			25	27.0
Threshold Adjustment				<5.4> (Less 20%)
TOTAL				**21.6**

167

Compare Job Opportunities

Score more than one job opportunity, and you are now ready to compare one opportunity against another. First, compare weighted totals. Then focus your attention on the most heavily weighted factors. Add up the weighted scores on these top-priority factors, and compare them from one job opportunity to another.

Your final decision table might look something like this:

Decision Factor	Weighted Score JOB#1	Weighted Score JOB#2	Weighted Score JOB#3
Boss	6	4.5	6
Role, etc	3	4.5	6
Products, etc.	3	2	4
Risk	2	2	2
Pay	5	3	2
Location	4	2	2
Career	3	3	4
Work hours	1	1.5	.5
SUBTOTAL	27.0	22.5	26.5
Threshold Adjustment	<5.4> (Less 20%)		
TOTAL	**21.6**	**22.5**	**26.5**

After this entire math exercise, you may be wondering where the flesh and blood of the jobs went to. Answer: right here. You're looking at a choice for Job #3 on the total weighted scores. But there is an even clearer choice for Job #3 when you look at the weighted scores for the top two factors. It is this top-priority total which tends to signal the most exciting job for you. Another way to get a handle on excitement from an organizational perspective is to ask yourself: "Can I see myself working happily in this company 5-10 years from now?"

As soon as you complete your first round of interviews, you should apply this method (or your own method) to the job opportunity. Granted, no one has yet offered you a job. But when someone does, timing becomes critical. It is unethical, for example, to make the offering company wait while you beat the bushes for competing offers. If you have other opportunities in the final stage, it is ethical to tell the offering company that you have one or two other opportunities, one or two other on-site or area visits, and that you will make a final decision by a certain date. Wait until just before that date to make any counteroffers.

Jim's Story

Note the reference to "on-site or area visits" in the previous paragraph. The Interview chapter discussed on-site visits. But what are area visits? If you are making the job decision with your family, and the job opportunity is out of town, I strongly advise a pre-decision trip to the area by you and your partner. During your interviews, you can state this necessity if things progress. Every time I have done this, which is several times, the prospective employer understood fully.

Once you make the decision and inform each company of the outcome, there remains one good deed to be done. You will be doing this good deed for yourself by reconnecting with each member of the network you have spent months creating and by closing the loop. You want to keep the network alive and breathing. A natural way to do this is to tell your contacts of your job decision, thank them for their help, and agree to keep in touch. Because some of these contacts may be looking for a job themselves in the near future, you might offer them whatever help you can in your upcoming position. Believe it: the contacts you sustain will come in mighty handy one day!

SUCCESS GAUGE
You have mastered D is for Decide if:
You have an objective evaluation method for determining which of several offers are right for you. You are prepared to follow this method. Extra points for scoring at least one job opportunity.

Conclusion

This book has been designed as an action guide for anyone who is looking for a GOOD job. By now, we can define a "good job" more precisely as:

- A job in your preferred career (see Step One: Reflection)
- A job consistent with your preferred job type (see Step Five: Purpose)
- A job that exceeds several – and meets virtually all – of the threshold scores for your most important decision factors (see Step Twenty-one: Decision)

This guide is effective only to the extent that you succeed in finding a GOOD job. Follow the steps, include the central characters in your life, stay focused, and your chances of landing a GOOD job are in your favor.

If are not finding success so far –if you have not interviewed on-site with at least one company after 90 days – try repeating the REST step. Should you choose a different career, it's a whole new search. Should you stay with the same career choice, you already have a valuable network. Consider investing another month in building that network. Do not give up. Remember: it's a big world out there, with job opportunities coming open all the time. Good luck!

Jim's Story

In my last job search, my first job offer came from one of my references on the 15th day of my search. The offer came close to my preferred job type, but did not fit it in one or two important ways. My second job offer came on the 66th day, and my third offer on the 91st day. I finally decided among these job opportunities on the 116th day, after my wife and I had visited two of the job sites.

The flowchart on the following page shows, by source, the numbers of contacts, responses, and interviews that led to my three job offers. By "job available" responses, I mean the portion of contacts or answered want ads which resulted in a headhunter describing an open position to me, or the manager behind a want ad calling me, or a targeted employer calling me back with the current or future possibility of a job. The reduction in numbers between "job available" responses and full-fledged telephone interviews was due to a job mismatch from my perspective, a mismatch from the company's perspective, or a job possibility too far in the future.

For me, this numbers game came to fruition three times. I know it will be an easier task for me to get a GOOD job next time, if there is a next time.

Kathy's Insights

I hope you have enjoyed our five steps to landing a GOOD job. Hopefully, you have used our guide over these three months to aid your transition. We hope you found value in the sequence of action steps and our straightforward approach to coach you to land a GOOD job. Please share our guide with your colleagues and relatives, and use it each time you prepare to make a career transition. Visit our website for ongoing career transition guidance and coaching.

MY JOB SOURCES

	HEAD-HUNTERS	NETWORK	TARGETED EMPLOYERS	WANT ADS / JOB SITES
CONTACTS	34 ↓	47 ↓	48 ↓	4 ↓
"JOB AVAILABLE" RESPONSES	16 ↓	7 ↓	4 ↓	2 ↓
TELEPHONE INTERVIEWS	8 ↓	3 ↓	0 ↓	1 ↓
ON-SITE INTERVIEWS	2 ↓	3 ↓	0 ↓	1 ↓
JOB OFFERS	1	2	0	0